DEF LEPPARD

NO SAFETY NET

CHRIS COLLINGWOOD

Published by Castle Communications Plc
Book Division, A29 Barwell Business Park
Leatherhead Road, Chessington, Surrey KT9 2NY

Copyright © 1994 Castle Communications Plc

Design: Brian Burrows
Paintings/Illustrations: Brian Burrows
Photographs supplied by: Redferns, Pictorial Press Ltd,
London Features International Ltd, Joe Bangay

Every effort has been made to find the copyright holders of the photographs in this book, but one or two were untraceable. We would be grateful if the photographers concerned would contact Castle Communications Plc (Book Division).

ISNB : 1 898141 55 X

DEF LEPPARD

NO SAFETY NET

CHRIS COLLINGWOOD

DEF LEPPARD • NO SAFETY NET

CONTENTS

IT WAS A THURSDAY...

Introduction

As usual in England this was the day that Sounds magazine was published. In the days before widespread rock music coverage in the media, Sounds was the only way to read about new rock bands, most of them covered by the paper's features editor Geoff Barton. On this particular Thursday in 1979 the paper had the second part of a feature called "The New Wave Of British Heavy Metal", a title coined by the paper's then editor Alan Lewis, and one which Barton was none too keen on. Whereas part one had featured a review of a show at London's Music Machine (later renamed the Camden Palace and turned into a dance club for the young and trendy), featuring a triumvirate of the then unknown Iron Maiden, Angelwitch and Samson; part two concentrated solely on one band, Sheffield's Def Leppard. Barton had gone to Sheffield to see a gig by the fledgling group and to interview them. The subsequent feature was so full of praise for the band's freshness of ideas, youth and sheer enthusiasm that people had to take notice. This was my introduction to the band. Strangely enough that same day, I was to go for an interview in the Covent Garden offices of Spotlight Publications, the publishers of Sounds, for a job as a messenger. I got the job, but the thing I remember most on being shown around the offices was a picture of Def Leppard lying in a filing tray; a picture that hadn't been used in the feature. It was of the band on stage, with Joe Elliot looking into the camera. The look on his face, screwed up and sweaty though it was, was of someone with supreme confidence, someone who seemed to know what fate had in store, even though at that particular time he couldn't possibly know how big they would become, or what price some of them would pay along the way. When I finally did get to hear them, via the three track ep that they released on their own Bludgeon Riffola label, they were everything Barton's article promised and more. Since they first started they may have lost a lot of the rawness that they had way back then, and they may have sometimes sounded like they're writing to a set formula, but somewhere in the stratosphere a huge rock machine is coming up with glorious riff after glorious riff for them. And yet, through all the good times and despite the bad times, they have firmly remained the same nice lads from Sheffield that they've always been.

It may not always have been fun, but its sure been interesting.

ACKNOWLEDGEMENTS

In writing this book I have tried to largely avoid the date of birth/favourite colour syndrome, and have also tried not to re-review songs that will have been heard hundreds and hundreds of times before by anyone who likes the band enough to read a book on them. What I hope that emerges is a book that shows the personal development of the band, and also takes in elements that were essential in their career growth, such as the rise of the NWOBHM. The majority of the material contained in this book is from my own personal recollections, and also the recollections of others that were involved somewhere along the way. I would like to thank the following for their help and encouragement in this project. Phil Scott, who saw it through two publishers and two Arsenal cup victories; Tim Collins and all at Microrent PLC for the equipment and tips on how to plug it in; Lawrie, Maggy, Phil and Kit; Mark Blake.

This book is dedicated to Charlton Athletic Football Club for times both good and bad, and Leigh Mayos for everything else.

EMPTY POCKETS, EMPTY BED

Chapter One

> "It's not talent. It's not looks.
> It's a state of mind."
> Neil Young

J oe Elliot always wanted to be in a band. He couldn't do much, maybe play a little guitar and bang the drums, but he was never going to be good enough to be a top class drummer and he certainly knew people who were streets ahead as a guitarist. But he reckoned his voice was OK, not brilliant, but good enough to get by as a singer in a small time rock band. Years later he would joke, even after years of success, that his voice was 'firing on all one' a reference to top class cars firing on all six (cylinders). He was also the only one with the front to be a singer. It was always the singer that bands were looking for, and when, in 1977, Pete Willis, Richard Savage and drummer Tony Kenning were looking for one, Joe was chosen for no other reason than willingness. The three of them had met at the youth club of Tapton School, which they all used to attend every Tuesday night. It was Willis who knew Joe, and also knew that he really wanted to be in a band. Willis reckoned Joe didn't have much of a voice, but he was tall and looked good with the microphone. At their first official rehearsal he sang Led Zeppelin's 'Stairway To Heaven' and David Bowie's 'Suffragette City', but completely flat, a whole octave down. But they stuck with it, even choosing the name Atomic Mass, although Elliot at the time thought this a bit of a stupid name. He had an imaginary band, one that he had made up during hours of daydreaming, and he'd even designed a logo. 'Deaf Leopard' was their name, and during a band meeting in his bedroom Joe persuaded the others that it was a better name than Atomic Mass. For a jokey homage to Led Zeppelin, who were originally called Lead Zeppelin but changed the spelling to avoid people pronouncing it Leed, he changed the spelling to Def Leppard.

The band carried on rehearsing, but always wanted another guitarist, particularly Willis. "I wanted a foil for my playing, and was a big fan of the two guitar bands such as Thin Lizzy. Plus, when playing live the rhythm tends to go during solos, and we always wanted to be the kind of band that has a full sound." On leaving school they got jobs, none of them with

any particular academic ambitions. They knew that they wanted the band to make it, and with the idealism of youth they just pondered on just how long it would take. Savage had a harder decision to make than the rest of them. Having been an exceptional footballer at school he was taken on trial by Sheffield United, arch rivals of the team he used to go and watch, Sheffield Wednesday. United offered him a contract which, after much thought, he turned down. "It was a tough choice" he reflected, "but not as tough as it would have been if it was Sheffield Wednesday offering me the contact. As far as I could see, even then, it was a straight choice between being a footballer or a musician, which thinking back might sound a bit arrogant." He opted instead to join British Rail as he had decided to be a musician and, unlike football, there isn't an instant apprentice wage for rock stars.

Joe, on the other hand, had gone to work on the shop floor for Smith Widdowson and Eadem Ltd, an ironmongery company in Sheffield. Peter Staniland, the then company secretary and whose son Andrew is now a playwright, remembers Joe as someone who seemed obsessed with music. He recalls being surprised when, years later, a Leppard video was on television and it was pointed out to him that the singer was the very same Joe Elliot. Willis became an apprentice lathe operator, Sheffield at the time being the steel capital of Europe. There was very little unemployment at that time, although since then Sheffield has been neglected by successive Governments with hardly any investment made in the city, resulting in only a proportion of the industry remaining. While training, Willis was required to attend Stannington College. It was here that he met Steve Clark. In the college library Willis was leafing through a guitar-effects manual. Clark spotted this and at the time was looking to join another band. He'd played with several locally, but they were always lacking ambition. "It seemed they wanted to play a bit so they could say they were in a band but really all they wanted to do was sit down the pub telling each other what they would do when they made it, instead of actually doing anything about it" he recalled later. Clark had first started playing the guitar at the age of eleven. His parents had resisted his pleas for a guitar for a while, but agreed that they'd get him one so long as he took classical guitar lessons. He did and would learn pieces by Vivaldi while at night playing along to records by Thin Lizzy and The Sensational Alex Harvey Band. Clark was particularly struck with SAHB's guitarist Zal Clemenson, who would play on stage in clowns make-up and sport a permanent fixed grin. Clark always admired his ability to make things look easy with the economy of his playing. Clark approached Willis and asked if he played, and Willis told him about the band. They both mentioned a few names of bands they listened to, lists that were fairly similar such as UFO and Judas Priest and Clark wondered whether they may need a second guitarist, but Willis, who even then had a reputation for aloofness, even though people who knew him well said that this was to compensate for his shyness, was fairly casual about it, eventually suggesting that Clark might want to drop in on a rehearsal sometime. Clark thought Willis didn't seem that bothered, and wondered whether maybe he was just someone else with a lack of ambition. He said he'd think about it.

A few nights later Judas Priest were playing at the Sheffield City Hall, and Clark once again bumped into Willis, this time with Elliot. In the bar Willis repeated the offer for Clark to come down, and this time he accepted. On January 29th 1978 in Bramall Lane, the band rehearsed with Clark for the first time in a garage/rehearsal room they'd found and used because it was the cheapest. Joe recalls it cost a fiver a week to hire, although Savage has since said he's not sure whether they ever paid the owner for it. They asked Clark what songs he knew, and he suggested they play Lynyrd Skynyrd's 'Freebird,' which had become a rock anthem, and which featured massive amounts of lead guitar playing. Clark handled the lead guitar parts himself, the others were suitably impressed and asked him to join straight away. What most impressed Clark was their commitment. "We'd go down the pub like the other bands had done before, but only at the end of the rehearsal. Also we'd rehearse every night, not just once a week and sit round talking about how great we were going to be one day." Joe remembers that even then they had a strong belief in themselves. "I remember one night in the winter of '78 me and Pete Willis were going home from rehearsal and we had enough money to either take the bus or buy a pint between us. We decided on a pint in a pub near Bramall Lane, huddled round the gas fire with a straw each. We walked home past Sheffield City Hall and I found some chalk and wrote 'Def Leppard will play here in 1980.'" They did so, and they sold it out.

From January to July the band rehearsed...and rehearsed ...and still rehearsed. "By now", said Clark "I was itching to gig. We were rehearsing for three hours a night but the others seemed happy to keep doing that. One night down the pub I said I'd had enough. I'd got a couple of pints inside me and threatened to quit the band if we didn't play a gig soon." To Steve's surprise the others said ok, that's fine, let's do it. "I remember being really shocked" he said, "and thinking I've done it now! I think it was the kick up the arse we needed. I just felt we could be there forever in that little rehearsal room!" The gig was duly booked, at Westfield school in Sheffield on July 18th 1978. The band smuggled in some beer in a bass drum, and at the end of the show one of the teachers at the school gave them five pounds from his own pocket

They performed a couple of covers, such as Bob Seger's 'Rosalie', but were by now writing their own songs.

The first song they ever wrote together was 'Sorrow Is A Woman', (originally titled 'Misty Dreamer') which even made its way onto their debut album. They then wrote 'War Child', a song that Joe reckoned made Black Sabbath sound like The Nolan Sisters, and 'Getcha Rocks Off', one which they all instantly thought was a bit special. In November of 1978, after only seven gigs the band decided they wanted to record something. Joe borrowed £148.50 from his father, also named Joe, and the band went to Hull to record three tracks. Before this however, the band had a change in line up.

Tony Kenning had started getting serious with his girlfriend Ann Brownbridge. She wasn't happy with his involvement in the group, reckoning that Tony thought more of them than he did of her. She issued him with an ultimatum, her or the band. He chose to stay with her, a decision he was to regret as they split up fairly soon after that. He told the band, who were obviously upset; but if someone didn't have enough commitment then fine, it was better that they left. This left them with a gap to fill for the recording of the ep, and they borrowed drummer Frank Noon who was later to play with Lionheart, the group formed by ex Iron Maiden guitarist Dennis Stratton and ex Tygers Of Pan Tang singer Jess Cox, and Stampede, who featured guitarist Laurence Archer who later went on to join the reformed version of UFO (featuring only Phil Mogg and Pete Way from the original band).

They recorded three tracks, 'Getcha Rocks Off', 'Ride Into The Sun' and 'The Overture'. This was released in January of 1979 on the bands own Bludgeon Riffola label. The name of the label comes from a review of the band when they supported The Human League in Sheffield. The Human League at the time were bleak industrialists who even then had silly hair cuts, and the decision to put the two bands on the same bill was a strange one. A review of this show slagged Leppard, describing their music as 'bludgeon riffola'. The band, rather than being upset, found this hilarious, and decided to revive the term for the name of the record label. "We figured that people would at least be aware of where we were coming from, that we had a sense of humour rather than being po-faced like the Human League."

The first 150 copies of the single, which was going to be the entire run, was released with a picture cover and a signed lyric sheet. These sold out, and the band quickly had more pressed. The entire run of this first release was 1,000 copies. To aid them with the selling of this single, Joe took copies around to local record shops. One of these was Revolution Records, run by Tony Martin.

At the time the recent punk 'do it yourself' revolution meant that independent recordings were very popular. Small eight and sixteen track studios were booming around the country as bands, particularly punk bands who had enthusiasm but couldn't really play, dashed to record something. Martin had loads of people bringing in singles to him, and adverts for the shop at the time boasted some of the strange stock that he was carrying. Most of these were destined to be something to laugh about ten years later, but Martin used to listen to them all. "I wasn't particularly a fan of punk," says Martin, "but I liked the enthusiasm and energy that the bands had." On playing Leppard's ep, Martin realised he had something more than just another souvenir. "I was really knocked out by it. They could really play, you could hear where the influences came from, but there was something so fresh about their sound that I couldn't quite put my finger on it." Martin was in contact with Frank Stuart-Brown, a pr man working mainly in the North of England, and had sent him a copy. When he heard it he immediately phoned Martin to try and get Joe's address. "I wanted to manage them" he remembers, "there was just so much potential there. England hadn't produced a decent hard rock band for years, what with the punk thing, and here at last was one practically screaming to be heard."

Martin wouldn't give him Joe's address, as he already had plans of his own for the band. The two of them talked and decided that they could work together, Martin handling the business side and Stuart-Browne looking after publicity. Leppard readily agreed, because apart from anything else the youth of the band meant it would probably be difficult for them to handle the business side of things. Joe had done most of it up till then, but it was almost like handing over control of the band to adults, and adults with contacts in the music industry at that. Whereas most bands at Leppard's level had a friend who would look after things for them, Leppard had a management COMPANY, as the two formed MSB (Martin-Stuart-Browne) Management.

Within months the two would be shown to be hopelessly out of their depth, but for the time being everything was rosy. Except that they needed a new drummer, so they advertised. One of the people who spotted their advert was Jeff Allen, whose fifteen year old son Rick was a drummer. Rick had been playing for years, even giving an interview about drumming at the age of twelve to The Sheffield Telegraph & Star. But Rick didn't really want to apply, saying he was getting sick of drumming and wanted to pack it all in, even though this could be seen as nothing more than a display of youthful petulance. In the end, tired of his sons unwillingness to phone, Jeff Allen called the number himself. It was arranged that Rick would go down to The

Limit Club in Sheffield and meet Joe and Steve. They chatted in the toilet and both of them were impressed enough with Rick to offer him the job there and then, without having heard him play. When he did go down to rehearse with them, it was obvious straight away that they had made the right choice, although Willis was initially surprised that they'd offered the gig to a schoolboy who they had never heard play. "Once we heard him though we were all amazed at how young he was. Apart from anything, he looked too weedy to be able to hit the drums that hard. Although we were only two or three years older he was still at school, which made a heck of a difference to us 'working men'. But it gelled immediately, it was pretty obvious that we'd been lucky to find someone as good as Rick."

The new management company re-released the ep, this time with the catalogue number MSB001- an early indication that the two were in it for personal glory. The line-up was complete, management was in place, now all that remained was for the word to spread.

INTO THE ARENA

A lthough Stuart-Browne has since claimed a lot of the credit for Def Leppard's early success, it was Joe who initially sent the tape to Sounds magazine. At the time, Sounds was the only magazine covering heavy rock, and the only writer who did this was Features Editor Geoff Barton, who has since gone on to edit Kerrang! magazine. Nowadays there are many different rock magazines, all with ten-fifteen regular contributors, so rock bands get covered constantly. Each month there are new bands to watch out for, ones who are going to be as big as x or heavier than y, and with superlatives heaped upon even the most mundane bands by writers who would dearly love to discover 'the next big thing'- and let's face it, who wouldn't?- that record companies and the public are much more difficult to convince. Nowadays if you want to discover something new to listen to there are many different shops specialising ONLY in heavy rock, radio shows that will play you fifteen new bands in the space of two hours, and MTV which, can be turned on and viewed 24 hours a day. In 1979 the only media outlet was Sounds which rarely featured more than one interview with a heavy rock band per week, so any band that got coverage was bound to make people sit up and take notice.

Barton had, and still has, an unsurpassed reputation as a judge of heavy rock. His championing of Kiss among others back in the seventies helped to break the band in the UK more than any amount of advertising could ever have done. He liked the tape so much that he agreed to go and see the band play in Sheffield, at Crookes Workingmans Club, on June 6th 1979. At the time the heavy rock scene in England had been in the doldrums. Punk had swallowed up a lot of the older groups, which was a neccessary thing at the time. Bands like Wishbone Ash and Uriah Heep hadn't released anything worthwhile for years, and most gig venues were dominated by punk or 'new wave' bands. Heavy rock bands could not get gigs, the pub scene being crowded with one chord wonders. In London, Def Leppard's most oft-mentioned contemporaries Iron Maiden had been having trouble getting gigs because they weren't punk, and were even booked a gig at the Roxy club in Neal Street, the punk club where The Clash and The Damned made their reputations.They didn't play it. but a poster was printed up advertising the gig which was to haunt the band a couple of years later when someone found a copy and accused Maiden of being 'former punks'. This incensed Maiden bassist Steve Harris, who in his own words "hated punk. How anyone can go on stage and be spat at was beyond me.

Some bird from RCA, 'orny bird like, booked the gig for us and stupidly got it advertised. I even went down there to check the place out and couldn't believe it. If we'd have gone there with the following we had, however small it was at time, there would have been a riot."

Maiden were featured in 'The New Wave Of British Heavy Metal-part one', a feature in Sounds that ran before Barton's Leppard piece done at Crookes. Whereas Maidens was a padded out gig review, featuring them, Samson (featuring their future vocalist Bruce Dickinson, then known as Bruce Bruce) and Angelwitch (terrible Black Sabbath copyists whose bassist Kev Riddles, once during a show threw his bass in the air and, mistiming his catch, knocked himself out cold); Leppard were to get a whole centre page spread just to themselves.

The feature showed a playful arrogance in the band, Elliot reckoning they were in the band so that girls would "look at our balls". Years later, when quizzed on this, he still maintained it was true. Barton was amazed at how good they were despite their age, and was also to mention Joe's puppy fat which he would not get rid of for a good few months, as well as his leather look trousers, the band still being too poor for him to afford real ones. The pictures that accompanied the piece showed how young they were, and also that Joe had been the victim of one of the illest advised perms since Kevin Keegan. Barton really gave the band his full seal of approval in the feature, which appeared in the issue dated June 16th, saying that they had a degree of tightness which is usually only attained after half a dozen American tours. He later felt he'd gone slightly over the top in his enthusiasm, but by now the whole of the record industry had sat up and taken notice. It also caused conversation at other bands gigs for quite a while after this, most notably the Led Zeppelin gigs at Knebworth on August 4th and 11th that year, with more than one camp fire conversation being between rock fans divided by thinking Leppard were either just an arrogant bunch of kids and those, like myself, who viewed them as a real breath of fresh air.

At Knebworth the ones who viewed them as upstarts tended to be the Deep Purple/Uriah Heep/Hwakwind fans, while the pro Leppards were the younger UFO and Thin Lizzy fans, the very bands that Leppard themselves listened to. (Strangely enough, Leppard also attended the Led Zeppelin gig. This was the day after, that they had signed a recording contract with Phonogram.) Another thing that had emerged from Barton's feature was the band were essentially fans, they were doing this because they loved music. Joe in particular had always been a huge music fan, even though the first single he ever purchased was the embarrassing choice of The

Archies bubblegum pop hit 'Sugar Sugar'. Whereas the others were more straight ahead rock fans, Joe was more influenced by lyricists like David Bowie and Mott The Hoople's Ian Hunter. He even took on board some of punk's more talented bands, realising that The Sex Pistols, The Clash and his own favourites The Doctors Of Madness gave bloated corporate rock a "good kick up the bum".

During the same week as the feature, Andy Peebles had been broadcasting a session on his Radio One evening show that the band had done, although by then they had already been played on Radio One by John Peel in his 10pm-midnight show which was almost exclusively new wave led, Peel being a champion in Britain for all the great post punk bands from Joy Division onwards. Peebles had first heard the band when he and his producer Geoff Griffin were being driven by Frank Stuart-Browne from Leeds to Manchester in the latters PR capacity, before he became full time Leppard manager. "Myself and Geoff were in the car and Frank said 'I've got a tape I think you should listen to'. This usually happens on such trips so you get used to it, but it can be embarrassing if the band turn out to be a load of rubbish, as they often do. But when you're in a car you are literally a captive audience, you can't get out even if you wanted to. We said OK and he put on what turned out to be the Def Leppard's ep. By the end of the tape both Geoff and I had agreed that we should offer this band a session. There were elements of early Yes there with an energy that I thought was just right for the kind of show we were trying to put together."

For MSB management, having the feature and the session was a masterstroke, although Stuart-Browne's later claim that he purposely co-ordinated this doesn't quite ring true. All of this activity had one affect; record companies were now clammering to see the band live. MSB decided that a show at the Retford Porterhouse in Nottinghamshire would be the ideal venue for Leppard to display their talents to record companies. One person who attended the show was Geoff Banks, a freelance writer then producing his own fanzine 'Teenage Depression. "We'd heard the ep and thought it showed a load of potential" he remembers. "I went along with two other people from the magazine who had decided to drive up to Retford from London to see them. We arrived slightly late but as soon as we walked in I couldn't believe the amount of record company people there. EMI, CBS (now Sony), Phonogram, Atlantic...they were just some of the people I recognised! The band seemed really nervous, and when I got chatting to them afterwards they told me that they knew how many record companies were meant to be coming, and that this had made them edgy. The last thing that you really want to do to a young band in their position is freak them out by telling them how they could fall flat on their faces if it's a bad gig." Banks remembers the gig as good, if not spectacular. "Some of the people from the record companies were the older guys, a couple of them fairly senior in A&R. They were the ones standing at the bar, and it was pretty obvious that they didn't think much of the band. It was the younger guys who seemed to be enjoying it."

This is something which was confirmed by Dave Bates, A&R man at Phonogram who was at the gig. He'd been looking for a young British rock band whom he felt would sell in America, and Leppard seemed tailor made for this, not least because by then they were playing a song called 'Hello America', a homage to all the places in America that Joe had read about, talking about 'Frisco, Hollywood and San Pedro Bay. "These were the places rock bands sang about" he recalled when asked about the lyrics."They just sounded so romantic. What did people want me to do, write a lyric about Cleethorpes and Doncaster?" It was a fair point, but one that in England was to soon get Leppard into trouble. Bates remembers how young they looked. "It was pretty obvious that the drummer hadn't ever shaved in his life, and come to think of it I don't think the bass player had either".

Despite, or maybe partly because of their youth and the way they would probably respond to 'suggestions' from record companies better than more mature musicians, he decided that they were indeed the band that he had been looking for, and so Def Leppard were signed to Phonogram. Rick Allen was still legally under age to sign anything, so his Dad signed the contract for him. The first thing Phonogram did was release the ep for a third time. By now it had sold 16,000 copies, including the initial 1,000 pressed, and went on to sell a further 14,000 on Phonogram.

By this time, Joe had become a regular vistor to London, and a regular visitor to see Geoff Barton at Sounds. It was here that I first met him, in my capacity as a messenger for Spotlight Publications. Having never met a real pop star, let alone one I was a fan of, I said (and I remember it clearly because of my cool demeanour) "You're that bloke in Def Leppard aren't you. Where'd you get your badge?" Joe was sporting a dinky white boot ceramic badge, similar to the one used as the cover for the 'Wasted' single, which was to be released in November '79. Seeing that I had a Rush badge on, Joe spoke of his fondness for them, and came across as very down to earth, something that never left him whenever we would (more and more sporadically) bump into each other through the years.

On one occasion the whole of the band trooped in, just because they were in London and decided to pay Barton a visit. They sat, somewhat self-consciously, round Barton's desk while the rest of the Sounds staff (for it was a fairly small office) looked on with mild amusement. After the group left one of the staffers was heard to mutter 'it's nice when children come and visit their dads at work', a reference to their youth. In September '79 Phonogram decided that it was time to get Leppard out on a nationwide tour prior to them recording their debut album. It was thought that it would be best to get them a support slot, one that would expose them to an audience who may not otherwise get to hear them. The choice was made for the band to support Sammy Hagar, latterly David Lee Roths replacement in Van Halen but then purely a solo artist. Hagar was, again with help from plenty of coverage in Sounds, gaining a good reputation in Britain, and Leppard were fans of Hagar from his work on Montroses' self titled debut album, which remains one of the all time classic hard rock albums. Not that the band had much say in the matter, but it was felt by the record company that Hagar, as a relatively new solo artist, would attract the type of audience that Leppard should be reaching.

The tour would be one night stands in established venues such as Hammersmith Odeon, and opened in September at Newcastle City Hall. The band were understandably excited, even if they were starting to feel unsure about MSB's management. It seemed to them that MSB were trying to protect them too much, but in a way that made them proprietorial rather than helpful towards the bands career. Rick Allen and Joe in particular were worried that MSB were getting out of their depth, and they started to feel that they had taken the band as far as they could with the ability they had as managers. Leppard were, after all, their first management project, so they had to learn 'on the job' rather than having the experience to know what to do next. "Some of the time" Martin was to admit later "It was a bit hit and miss, but we always had the band's best interests at heart." Many observers around the band didn't agree, and more than one person at their record company at the time wanted MSB not to be involved with Leppard any more.

Things were really to come to a head on the way to that first gig with Hagar.

ENTER THE HOT SHOT YANKS

For a while, Leppard's progress had been monitored by Peter Mensch, who was with the giant Leber-Krebs management company in the States, and who handled the affairs of Ted Nugent and AC/DC, among others. His partner, Cliff Burnstein was A&R Man at Mercury Records in New York, a division of Polygram Records. Burnstein had been sent a tape of the band from London and was told they had been signed. Burnstein told Mensch that he had to get hold of them for management. Mensch was a man with a reputation, a clever man, a man who was normally right on the button. Mensch, unlike far too many rock managers, was a massive music fan, and was instrumental in reviving the career of ex UFO guitarist Michael Schenker, who had left the band in a haze of too many drugs and joined the Moonies. On more than one occasion Mensch would say that Schenker was a real hero to him, the best guitar player he'd ever heard, and that revitalising his career was as much of a pleasure for him as it was for the fans to hear Schenker playing again. Both the music business realist and rock fan in him told him that Def Leppard had something very, very marketable. But they were with another management company and Mensch thought well, I can't approach them. Except....

Except that on the way to the gig at Newcastle City Hall, Joe Elliot had a fist fight with one of the management team. Rick Allen, still two years off the legal age to drink in Britain, had taken a litre bottle of cheap wine with him. And drunk it. All of it. But not in a 'yeah I'm a big rock star now' way. For Rick, this was the equivalent of a school trip, being away from your parents for a few days, and a licence to drink.

Not surprisingly, the mixture of a litre of wine and the swaying motion of the coach resulted in Rick, in his own words, 'spewing his ring up.' Pete Martin ordered Andy Smith, who was driving the bus at the time, to clear Rick's sick up, and Andy naturally refused. Joe, feeling that if Rick was going to be sick he should take the consequences for his actions, stuck up for Andy, and a heated argument ensued, resulting in Joe and Martin coming to blows just before they went on stage. Joe remembered it as a kind of final straw. "It would have happened anyway. I just felt that these people didn't have a clue anymore, but were so desperate to look like they knew what they were doing and were big time management that we were being held back." Remembering the incident a year or so later, Willis remembered watching in horror as the two started physically assaulting each other. "I couldn't believe it. Just before a gig in front of the biggest crowd we'd ever played to and they were fighting. It seems so stupid when you think about it, quite funny really, but at the time it was really upsetting. Joe was always the loudest band member, so really he was just voicing our frustrations. The timing could have been a bit better though." Despite this, the tour was a major success for the band.

At the Hammersmith Odeon show, the whole venue was full in time to see the band, whereas the norm at this particular venue was to wait until the headliners were about to come on as the theatre's arcane management did not allow you to take drink into the auditorium. Before the show myself and some friends were hanging around the stage door, as one of them was a huge Sammy Hagar fan since his Montrose days. Joe came out and, seeing me, came over to say hello. That he recognised someone he'd met briefly a couple of times was a surprise, but he stood and chatted for a while about the tour and how friendly everyone from Hagar's organisation had been to them. Leppards show was stunning, the band making full use of the Hammersmith stage. Hagar had indeed been generous to them, as the band had a very full sound, with Clark even employing 'speaker to speaker' during 'Answer To The Master'. This involved the riff he played during the middle section of the song being transferred from one speaker stack to another. This hadn't always worked, and on one occasion earlier in the tour no noise came from either speaker, somewhat ruining the dramatic atmosphere of the song.

Joe still had his puppy fat, and his by now real leather trousers did him no favours sartorially, but the energy that they put into the performance was real, and they came across as a band genuinely excited to be performing live. Rick Allen even did a drum solo, which sounded too similar to Rush's Neil Peart in some places, but the economy with which they had increasingly employed in their songwriting-as Joe said at the time, "people are sick of fifteen minute keyboard solos" – came across in this too, so the solo was kept fairly short.

In the bar after they'd played, most people were impressed, although criticism was once again aimed at their perceived cockiness. This came, as was becoming the norm, from fans of the older generation of rock bands. It was as if the argument was that they hadn't 'paid their dues', that they'd been plucked from school and given a fabulous recording contract without first playing all the toilets around the country thirty-four times. It was an argument that was to be heard all too frequently over the coming months.

Following the Hagar tour Mensch, now hot on the band's trail and desperate to manage them, arranged for them to be the support act on the November British tour by one of his charges, AC/DC. To coincide with this, Phonogram released the first 'proper' Leppard single 'Wasted' b/w 'Hello America.' Produced by Nick Tauber, this unfortunately did the band no justice at all. Although the material was strong, the production was too poppy and light, with the main riff in 'Wasted' sounding as if it was being played through a six watt amp.

NO SAFETY NET

This was to be AC/DC's last British tour with frontman Bon Scott, who died in London a few months later, after a heavy nights drinking. This tour was of the same type of venues as their previous support slot, but AC/DC were much more popular than Hagar, so they could easily sell out two nights at Hammersmith Odeon without help from a name support band. Once again Leppard got treated very well, although Joe remembers AC/DC, apart from Scott, as being very quiet and shy. During the tour Leppard decided that enough was enough with MSB and Rick Allen approached Peter Mensch asking for his help, and intimated that the band would be interested in Mesch taking over their management.

This was of course what Mensch wanted, but he was worried by the ethics of the situation. Allen asked him to listen in to what MSB were doing to the band; and Mensch subsequently overheard conversations between MSB and the band that he could not believe. He and Burnstein decided that, for the good of the band, MSB had to go. And so with the band greatly relieved, they set about a long legally protracted (and expensive) battle to get Leppard away from them.

Years later, when questioned on the ethics of their actions, Burnstein would say "is it ethical to let a band with that much talent drown because the people who handle them haven't got what it takes?" This is a fair point, but one which left MSB seething. Stuart-Browne had seen the band as his meal ticket to the top, and he had started viewing himself as a major player. He has since said that the whole episode taught him a great deal. "I'd never trust anyone in business again, that's for sure" he said. The truth was that most people were actually pleased for the band. It was always known that they had it in them to crack America, and with Leber-Krebs management in place this became, if not a formality, a distinct possibility.

Late in 1979 Radio One broadcast an 'In Concert' session by the band, as well as one by Sammy Hagar. It was a fair representation of them at the time, opening with the long forgotten 'Glad I'm Alive'. At the end of the year Radio Times magazine had the Radio One disc jockeys run through their 'tips for the top' in 1980. Andy Peebles, not surprisingly, chose Leppard, and a rather tacky picture of them appeared, as if in a crystal ball, with Peebles looming over them. Interestingly enough, John Peel's opinion was that "anybody" could make it, and he chose to fill his crystal ball with a picture of Sounds messenger Richard Newson to illustrate this fact. Under a variety of aliases, Newson did go on to be a successful rock journalist, and wrote about Leppard on more than one occasion.

In December of 1979 Def Leppard were to go into Startling Studios in Ascot to begin work on their debut album with producer Tom Allom, who had previously worked with Leppard faves Judas Priest. They had every reason to think that, on the eve of a new decade, their popularity could only be in the ascendency.

ON THROUGH THE NIGHTMARE

Chapter Four

T he album took less than a month to record, and the band finished in the studio on January 5th 1980. It was due for a March release, and Phonogram had planned a meticulous and gruelling campaign to get the band noticed in Britain. Straight after recording the album they set out on their first headlining British tour, taking in medium sized venues such as London's Marquee, then based in Wardour Street. At the Boat Club in Nottingham, capacity about 300, nearly 400 people were turned away at the door, and it was a similar story all round the country. The band were supported by Witchfynde, a mediocre Midlands combo who were one of the bands being dragged along by the rock resurgence led by talented bands such as Leppard and Iron Maiden, Sounds' coverage of the NWOBHM, and the huge switch from pubs booking exclusively punk bands to also booking metal bands initiated. Witchfynde were really just Black Sabbath clones, and poor ones at that, but their Rondolet debut single 'Give 'Em Hell' was making an impression in the Indie charts, so they were also pulling in a few fans of their own. The Marquee gig was also the first review I was lucky enough to have published in Sounds magazine, as my by now constant pestering of Geoff Barton had worn him down enough for him to give me a chance to write.

The Marquee show opened with 'It Could Be You', then completely new to the crowd. Joe was by now coming to terms with how to dress (or being guided a bit more) and wore a white silk shirt with the leather trousers. I said they were 'as faultless as a young band could be', Rick Allen's 'rather disjointed' drum solo being the only exception. They played most of the forthcoming album, and Joe once again showed his sense of humour by announcing "about a year ago we released an EP with one track on it which has become very popular", obviously referring to 'Getcha Rocks Off', which by that time was attaining major status as a new rock anthem. The band instead played 'Ride Into The Sun' the least popular track on the EP, and the only track which they would not re-record on their debut album. They saved 'Getcha Rocks Off' till last, and the crowd ended up kneeling on the stage, playing formation air guitar.

Afterwards, Joe viewed the show as a triumph. He was really pleased that the band had done so well at The Marquee, as so many of his heroes such as David Bowie had started their career there. After this tour they immediately booked another one for March/April, this time of slightly larger

venues such as the 2,000 capacity Lyceum in London's West End. This tour would coincide with the album's release. To preceed this, Phonogram released 'Hello America' as a single on 21st Feb. With it's aforementioned embrace of the USA and the picture cover featuring the Statue Of Liberty, the single made the song sound much slicker than it had live, maybe a bit too overtly commercial, some said a bit too....Americanised.

The song made the top fifty, and Leppard were asked to appear on the British television show 'Top Of The Pops'. The show was at that time completely mimed, and Leppard were asked to mime their bit before transmission. Sadly, the song was never shown on the show, as the very day it was due to be broadcast the Space Shuttle was launched for the first time and the preceeding programme, a science programme, overran. Leppard, with the least successful single of the seven acts due to appear that week, were dropped. The producer, Robin Nash, told them that if the single went any higher they would show the song the next week, but it dropped out of the top 50, meaning Leppard would have to wait a while before their Top Of The Pops debut. Better news for the band were the results of the Sounds readers poll for that year. They had won both the 'Best New Band' and 'Best Single' categories. Their debut album, not due for release until March 14th, was reviewed in Sounds by Geoff Barton, who gave it a somewhat lukewarm review. Following the results of the poll, and with the album imminent, it was also decided that he would do another feature on the band for Sounds, again travelling up to Sheffield, this time to the Top Rank Club.

The band were to feature on the front cover of the issue dated 1st March. However, the caption on the cover was 'Has the Leppard changed it's spots?' Inside, Barton expressed his concern that Leppard had indeed sold out to America, that they'd placed their complete trust in the music business, and this has rendered them 'useless'. He felt that 'since signing a major deal, Def Leppard have begun to sink slowly into the record industry quagmire.' The band were shocked by this, as their former champion had seemingly turned against them. He would later acknowledge that he was too harsh on the band in this feature, but said that he had felt betrayed by them. "I felt like I'd been used as a stepping stone in the bands career, whereas I thought we'd actually built up a relationship", he recalled later. This article did damage the band's career in Britain, but probably not as much as the band thought, but at around the same time, without their knowledge, things were beginning to happen for them in America.

Cliff Burnstein had given a promo copy of the album to disc jockey Gloria Johnson,from station Q105 in Portland, Oregon. Johnson,whom Burnstein had known since the mid seventies, was a major hard rock fan. She realised that Leppard could be massive in America, and not knowing any history of the band took the album at face value, which was difficult for British fans at the time to do, and she began to play selected songs from it on her show, starting with 'Hello America', which got a positive response from her listeners.

In Britain, 'On Through The Night' was released on 14th March 1980, and entered the album charts at number 10. Just before this, Iron Maiden's debut LP had entered at number 4, so the inevitable comparisons between the bands- both young, both big music fans who were teaching the older bands that they could no longer rest on their laurels, both signing big record contracts around the same time (Maiden had signed to EMI) meant that, in Britain, Maiden were winning. The album featured eleven tracks, including the re-recordings of 'Getcha Rocks Off', now reduced to just 'Rocks Off', and 'The Overture'. The version of 'Rocks Off' was supposedly live, and featured terribly dubbed crowd cheering and lacked all the excitement of the original. The LP version ended with Joe in a mock American accent saying "Thang-kyoo! Goodnide! Woo-hoo!" which was very badly misjudged. The production on the whole album was very poor, Tom Allom taking out any rough edges and replacing them with something that was nearly, well, slick and Americanised. While he'd beefed up the riff of 'Wasted', he'd made the chorus sound like it was being sung through a megaphone in the next room. All the songs that had sounded so powerful live, such as the album opener 'Rock Brigade', 'Answer To The Master' and 'When The Walls Came Tumblin' Down', which featured probably the best lyrics Joe had written so far, were toned down. Whether Allom, who is not a wimpy producer, had a brief to bring out the slickness in the band is unclear, but the result was a real disappointment. Not that it was a bad album, it's just that it seemed they were capable of a lot more.

What really upset British rock fans though was the cover of a big American truck carrying a guitar. It wasn't the naffness of it, it just seemed the confirmation of everything that Geoff Barton had written. Barton hadn't started the 'Def Leppard have sold out to America' backlash, it would have come anyway. He just aired the opinions that a lot of people had at the time, myself included. Unfortunately for the band, he'd aired them in the major rock magazine in the country....

The other big shock, for MSB management at least, was that they were not thanked on the sleeve. They felt, even after the relationship had turned sour, they had still put a lot of work into Leppard and the band could have at least said thank-you on the sleeve of their debut album. "That really hurt" Stuart-Brown was to say later. "I know we had our problems but I'd have thought the band would have been adult enough to at least realise that we'd had their best interests at heart. We came out of it ok financially, and it didn't do us any harm business wise as far as other things go. But it will always rankle."

The tour continued into April, with support coming from The Tygers Of Pan Tang, who had just signed a deal with MCA Records after success on the North East of England based independent label Neat. Rob Weir, then the Tygers guitarist, now working for a legal firm in Newcastle, said at the time that although he thought Leppard would be around for a few years, a lot of fans weren't that keen on them. "I remember one gig in Wolverhapton" he said after the tour, "and while Leppard were on loads of people were coming down to our dressing room and telling us they were just a bunch of kids, that they were posing too much for their own good."

Despite this, the tour was a success, and Leppard, although severely scolded by Barton's criticisms, were looking forward to their first visit to America, where they were due to go in mid May in support of Ted Nugent. They were in America for eleven weeks in total. That was it. Back home, the storm that had been brewing ever since Barton's article was about to come to a head.

West Ham v Sheffield United.
Iron Maiden's Steve 'Chopper'
Harris joins Joe for a charity kickabout.

When Leppard, who'd had a tiring but rewarding time during their American travels, returned to Britain they had three weeks off to rehearse and write some new songs before they were due to appear at the Reading festival as the second to last band before Whitesnake on the third and final day. Even though they'd had warning signs, the band were still, quite rightly, looking forward to playing Reading. 1980 was, bar two or three bands, exclusively heavy rock, and almost anyone who's name had ever been mentioned under the banner NWOBHM, or who's career had been revived because of the resurgence in interest in heavy rock, was there. Samson, UFO, Krokus, Gillan (featuring ex Deep Purple singer Ian Gillan), Iron Maiden, Sledgehammer, Tygers Of Pan Tang ...the list is seemingly endless,and the bands names all seemingly ridiculous. On the Saturday, the night before Leppard were due to play, Maiden had played a triumphant set, culminating in guitarist Dave Murray leaping from the drum riser right to the front of the stage, and were by popular consensus the best band of the festival so far. Leppard were due to play straight after the debut appearance of Ozzy Osbourne's new band, Blizzard Of Oz, featuring the late Randy Rhoads.

Ozzy however pulled out of the festival and the early seventies pop band Slade were put in his place. Slade played an absolute blinder, going down brilliantly with the crowd who, at an average age of 18-19, would have been just the people who bought Slade's singles when they were a regular fixture on 'Top Of The Tops', between 1972 and 1976. Slade had kept playing through the lean years after the singles had dried up and, being seasoned musicians, knew exactly what to give the crowd. They played all their old hits, including 'Cum On Feel The Noize' which was to be such a massive hit for the appalling American heavy band Quiet Riot in 1983. It would have been difficult enough for Leppard going on after Ozzy, but after Slade the crowd were in the mood for a party. Instead, they got Leppard being cocky, arrogant, young, good looking, and Joe Elliot dressed not in leather and spandex, or even imitation leather and silk, but red baggy trousers...and a t-shirt with hearts on it...and a white cotton jacket. This was not HEAVY METAL.

Almost from the moment they came on stage, things were thrown at them. At Reading, it was always traditional to have a can/bottle/mud/anything you can throw fight among the crowd. Sometimes the sky was just full of debris flying backwards and forwards over the crowd. But occasionally bands got it too, usually only one or two things, but sometimes a lot. Def Leppard, and in particular Joe, got a lot. A full can of coke hit him straight in the balls, and throughout the set the stage piled up with rubbish.

It was an embarrassing sight, and all credit to the band for not walking straight off the stage, which they would have had every right to do. Backstage during Leppard's set, where I repaired to because a) I felt sorry for the band and b) I didn't want to get hit on the head by a bottle, which I thought was fair enough, Peter Mensch and Geoff Barton were having a fairly heated argument, Mensch accusing Barton of being the catalyst for what was happening to them, and Barton protesting his innocence and trying to calm Mensch down.

What was surprising was that neither the band nor anyone round them could see this coming. Everyone seemed genuinely surprised by it when, although amazed at it's severity, it was fairly obvious to others it would happen. Apart from anything else they just looked too cool, too...Americanised. Part of the problem was that it became part of the thing to do, and more than one person who I subsequently spoke to who was throwing stuff said it was because everyone else was. Since then, Britain has discovered you can be cool flash and make good music, witness the embrace of Bon Jovi who would have received the same treatment as Leppard did in 1980 had they been British and, it could be argued, would never have made it so big in this country had Leppard not blazed a trail for their kind of catchy hard rock. But in the climate of 1980 in Britain, heavy rock bands were meant to look, well, heavy. Denim and Leather. What would work well for them in America (their looks, their youth) counted greatly against them in Britain. British rock fans liked their heroes to look mean, like Motorhead's Lemmy. People like him, Hawkwind's Dave Brock and Uriah Heep's Mick Box -a man who invested the money he made from early Heep albums such as 'Look At Yourself' in a chain of launderettes just as everyone was buying washing machines- were how people should look. Def Leppard, to the average British punter, were too young (not their fault), too cocky (but they'd always been), and too handsome (better looking than most of them). For the first time in their career, Leppard were down in the dumps. It wouldn't be the last.

THE WAITING GAME

T hroughout September the band toured Europe, returning to the UK at the beginning of October to, they hoped, start work on their second album. This time they had chosen Robert John Lange, a South African known to one and all as Mutt, whose wife, Stevie, was best known in Britain for singing the accompanying song on a deodorant commercial. He'd actually been the choice to produce the first album, but was unavailable. He'd worked with Peter Mensch before, among other things producing AC/DC's eight million selling album 'Back In Black', their first after the death of Bon Scott. Mensch knew that he could get the sound that the band needed. As it turned out, Lange was still working on Foreigner's latest release, the album which was to become 'Foreigner 4', so was not ready for Leppard. The band were prepared to wait though, and in Mensch and Burnstein they had managers who were, if anything, more prepared to wait for Lange than they were.

By November Foreigner's album was still not completed, and rumours began to leak out about why. One was that Mick Jones, the bands songwriter, had been listening to too much 'new' music, so instead of writing the AOR that the band were famous for started producing neat, concise tunes that, although good, would not appeal to Foreigner's audience. Another rumour concerned Jones's private life, that his wife would only allow him to work from 9 to 5 each day. Whatever the reasons, Leppard were getting bored with sitting around. Joe and Pete attended a couple of gigs on the UFO tour in October, including one at the Apollo Theatre in Oxford. They'd gone there with the guitarist from Girl, a friendly Londoner called Phil Collen, a former alarm fitter who Joe said was a brilliant player but was wasting his talents in his current band. Girl were a glam/heavy rock band who were seen by many as desperate New York Dolls wanabees. They had been signed to Jet Records, home of Ozzy Osbourne and also the label run by notorious music business hardman Don Arden. Their first release had been a song called 'My Number', which was promoted at the special price of 49 pence (this when an average single cost 75 pence) in see-through clear vinyl. Singer Phil Lewis, who went on to successfully front LA Guns, was the subject of many an interesting tale, including that his parents were either English nobility or dead, depending on who was telling the story. The truth, as ever, was much more dull, his father being a newspaper vendor who lived in a fairly run down flat near Lancaster Gate in London.

Girl were all fairly good looking, and this got them a cult following in Japan almost immediately, the Japanese then being suckers for, as the Japanese magazine 'Music Life' said, "very pretty Western boys." Lewis's dad would always say to Japanese women buying a paper from him 'My son is Phil Lewis, you know him?' Which, of course, they never did. One night in The Ship, a pub just up the road from the old Marquee where the beer was flat, the toilets were filthy and the landlord would throw people out just for chewing gum- but hey, everyone went there! Joe and Pete spoke to Geoff Banks about the wait for Lange. Banks thought they should chuck it in and get someone else, but, even before they had worked with him, Pete and Joe spoke in awed terms about the technology he was employing, such as linking up two 32 track multi-track recorders just to get one guitar sound. They also defended their debut against criticism of its 'poppiness', saying they never wanted to produce a simple heavy metal album, and that accusations that it was produced with America in mind were 'utter garbage'.

With time on their hands, they decided to tour England in the December, taking in small venues including the old favourite the Retford Porterhouse. Partly it was to alleviate their boredom, but also to attempt to get back some street credibility. They felt that if the public saw them at small venues they may warm to them again, and the tour even took in a venue called Chesterfield's Aquarius, where you'd be more likely to see out of tune nightclub acts performing the hits of the sixties rather than the country's best young heavy rock act. But the tour was a disaster. Whereas at the beginning of the year Nottingham Boat Club had been well over subscribed, this time they had a total audience of 87 people. In Doncaster they had to cancel the show because of low advance ticket sales. The whole mood of the band was down, and Lange was still no nearer completing the Foreigner album. It was not to be until May that they could at last start working with Lange on a follow up to 'On Through The Night.' That the band, its management and the record company were prepared to wait for so long testifies to the confidence they had in Lange.

If Leppard had been bored, they were just about to find out what hard work really was. Lange was, and is, a perfectionist. The album was to be recorded at Battery Studios in North London's Willesden Green, which was where Iron Maiden had recorded their debut album. Lange told the band not to fall in love with anything they had written, as everything would be changed around. The way Lange worked took Leppard completely by surprise, but he later said he was just testing them out. "At the time I really liked the band's music, but didn't know how far they were prepared to go. Also we only had three months to do the album.

Looking back it was the real beginning of my relationship with the band. We were both testing each other out, seeing how far we could go. I tend to be very autocratic when I'm in the studio, but as it was the first time I'd worked with them I wasn't sure how much they were prepared to give."

Once they realised just how spot on Lange's ideas were, the band were prepared to give it all. "Mutt Lange completely changed the way we wrote things" said Joe later." We went in to the 'High And Dry' sessions thinking we had a set of really good songs together. We'd had enough time to write them, after all. People say Mutt is a disciplinarian to work with, but I just think he's disciplined. Lange felt that a lot of the time Pete Willis wasn't responding to the things Lange asked him to do, and on more than one occasion tore into him in front of the rest of the band. Willis had been having problems with his drinking for some time, and this was starting to affect him in the studio. He was basically very shy, and drinking made it easier for him to get on stage and throw all of the right shapes. The problem was it also made him belligerent and argumentative. The band had realised he had a problem the very first time they went to America, back in 1980. According to Joe, "He got on the plane this normal quiet bloke and got off nine hours later absolutely bolloxed. At the time it was almost funny, because we'd never really seen him like that before. We had to practically carry him off. It was when we realised that it wasn't an isolated incident that we started to worry."

'High'n'Dry' was released in the summer of 1981, and was an absolute revelation. The band themselves had every confidence in it, and although they knew that it wouldn't be a huge seller at first in Britain because of the way they were viewed, they still knew it would do ok because, as Savage said at the time, "Stuff the politics. It's what's in the grooves that counts. If it's good enough people will buy it no matter who it's by." Lange had indeed bought out the best in the band. Gone was the sheen of the first album, instead Leppard had captured all the good elements of their harmonic rock without losing any excitement. Right from the opening 'Let It Go' they sounded like they were coming back angry, as if they'd thought 'alright, we've been slagged off, people are saying we're too polished, that we've become American Adult Orientated Rock, well try THIS." In particular Allen's drum sound had been revolutionised, taking them from the bland backbeat sound they had on the first album to the powerhouse basis for all the songs. Lange had also changed the way Savage played the bass, as there was now a constant thudding rhythm not unlike that of AC/DC's bassist Cliff Williams, another Lange prodigy. The cover was also an improvement. Designed by Hipgnosis who had planned the weird and wonderful covers for, among others, UFO, it

featured someone just about to land in a swimming pool, while around the edge of the cover a crowd of bald men all dressed in leather jackets look to the skies. When asked at the time what it meant Joe retorted "Fucked if I know. All I know it's a big improvement on the first one. People can't say we're selling out to America with this cover, although knowing our luck they'll say all the baldies are Americans." The back cover also featured a thanks to 'You, for your patience'. If only they'd have known....

Britain remained unconvinced about the album, not because of a lack of faith in the material, but most people didn't bother to listen to it. The album only entered the UK charts at number 26, and sales soon dropped off. But they remained steady for quite some time, and as more people got to hear the album the strength of the material made them put aside their prejudices. In August 'Let It Go' was released as a single, backed another track from the album 'Switch 625'. They toured Britain, playing one nighters at the larger halls, including their first headlining show at the Hammersmith Odeon. They were still capable of selling these places out on their own, and a three band bill also comprising Lionheart and Atlantic Records big hopes MORE was put together. Geoff Banks attended several of the shows on this tour, as he'd struck up a good friendship with MORE. He remembers that Leppard seemed to keep to themselves. "It wasn't that they were unfriendly, they just seemed quite quiet. MORE and Lionheart would be up drinking half the night but Leppard used to disappear fairly early. Then again, they had a lot more to lose than the other two bands who were trying to establish a reputation while Leppard were fighting to regain theirs."

Halfway through the tour Phonogram decided that the band should cut their first videos, and hired the Royal Court Theatre in Liverpool. Leppard mimed to three songs from the 'High'n'Dry' album, 'Let It Go' 'Bringin' On The Heartbreak' and the title track itself. To give the shoot some atmosphere, members of the Def Leppard fan club were bussed in from Sheffield. The three songs took a day to shoot, and the crowd were given the chance to get autographs afterwards. For the shoot, Rick Allen wore Union Jack shorts, something which appealed to the band as another way of proving they were 'proud to be British'. It was a concept they were later to take a lot further. 'Let It Go' worked particularly well, one cut at the beginning shooting between Willis seemingly kick starting the riff to Clark's shambling stage moves, hunched over his guitar. But the one that had the most long term effect for the band was 'Bringin' On The Heartbreak.' This was sent to a fledgling company in America known as Music Television, or MTV, who started programming the video.

It was in this way that Leppard would initially get known to the non concert goers that constitute so much of the American album buying market (this is down to nothing more than the size of the country) and pave the way for the success they were soon to enjoy.

Pete Willis' drinking was getting more and more difficult for the band to handle. At one stage during the tour Joe rang his old friend Phil Collen and asked him whether he could learn sixteen songs in three days as the band were fed up with Willis. Collen said he could ("I lied" he was later to say). Girl had just finished a Sunday night residency at The Marquee which was attracting fifty fans and three hundred hangers on. "Some of our gigs were like parties where all the people you didn't want to be there had turned up. We had fun, sometimes it was a real laugh, but by mid '81 it was starting to be obvious that we were never going to make it big, so I was always on the lookout for other things." The next day Willis seemed repentant, and Joe called Phil to tell him he wasn't needed. Yet.

The show that year at Hammersmith Odeon was absolutely stunning. Both Lionheart and MORE had gone down really well with the crowd, and when Leppard came on there was a real feeling of 'come on then big shots, show us what you can do.' They opened with 'Another Hit And Run' and just floored the audience. Leppard were attacking the crowd and didn't pause for the first four numbers. Months of rehearsal, harking back to the early days of the band, plus the way Lange had shaken up their playing had given them back whatever confidence they had lost from their recent experiences. The band were, in the words of one review at the time, 'tighter than a duck's arse.' It was to be the start of their resurgence in Britain.

They spent the rest of 1981 touring both Europe and the USA, for some of the time in support of Judas Priest. Christmas was spent at home. 'High'n'Dry' was starting to pick up sales in America, but still mainly to audiences who had seen them live. They were now in the position of having to write what is known as 'that difficult third album,' when a band has used up all the standards they were doing before they get a record contract but needs to prove that they have the talent to forge a long term career. One of Leppard's main rivals, Saxon from Barnsley in Yorkshire had failed to do this, and it was a lesson that Joe in particular looked at. Saxon had produced the massively popular (in Britain at least) 'Wheels Of Steel' as their second album at around the same time that Leppard had released 'On Through The Night' and, or so Joe felt, stolen a lot of Leppard's thunder. But their third album had been weak, and by the end of 1982 Saxon were trying desperately hard to come up with something anthemic, when all that happened was they became an almost comedy Metal band. In 1982, when looking for material for a heavy metal parody movie they were to be writing and starring in, American actors Christopher Guest, Michael McKean and Harry Shearer would see a performance by Saxon which they later said was 'a major source of inspiration'. The film they made was 'This is...Spinal Tap', which has gone on to become a staple video on tour buses the World over.

Not that Leppard thought the same fate would befall them, as they once again secured the talents of Mutt Lange as producer. At the end of '81 Joe reflected on the year. "I feel ten times happier about things than I did this time last year, especially in Britain. We're still proud of the first album, but have to admit 'High'n'Dry is in a different league. We've already got some ideas for the next one which we reckon will really surprise people."

Def Leppard spent the first month of 1982 writing material for the next album, and pieced it together during the month of February. They linked up with Lange at Park Gate Studios at Battle, near Hastings in Sussex, England. Savage said he found the atmosphere there "Relaxing. It's such a quiet place that there's not the distractions there would be in a city. The only diversion from recording was the World Cup, the finals of which were taking place in Spain. Everything stopped for an important match." They recorded all of the backing tracks here, but by now Willis' reliance on alcohol had stretched the band to its limit. Joe reckoned he'd become a pain in the arse. "Pete wasn't any fun to be in a band with any more. We'd given him a last chance twenty or thirty times." They decided that he had to go. "They called me up" recalled Peter Mensch, "And said I had to get rid of him. At one time or another every member of the band has wanted to get rid of this or that member, but Pete was arguing with Mutt, something he was in no position to do." Lange remembers Willis turning up at the studio so drunk he couldn't play. "I thought he was joking. He tried to find a chord and he couldn't focus. I told him to go home and sober up."

Mensch refused to sack Willis saying that the band should do it. He reasoned that Willis was a founder member and the other people who he'd been with all that time should tell him. They agreed, and on World Cup Final day, June 1982, Pete Willis was sacked. For the band, there could only be one replacement. A couple of weeks before the news of Willis's sacking became public, Phil Collen was in the toilet of The Ship in Wardour Street. Chatting to a friend, he was asked whether he was going to join Leppard. "No mate, where'd you hear that?" He replied with a grin. His grin betrayed him.

Willis had already completed the backing tracks, and the band wanted to move to their old haunt, Battery Studios in London, to do the overdubs and the mix. Collen went down to the studio for a couple of days just to hang around, and the band gave him a tape of one of the songs from the forthcoming album, 'Stagefright.' Mutt asked him to go away and work out a solo for it. He returned the next day and played the solo, which would be the one that actually ended up on the record. Peter Mensch, who also knew and liked Collen, had wanted Mutt to test him out to see what he thought of him. Mutt reported to Mensch that not only could Collen play, he was probably better than anyone else in the band. On being asked to join, Collen replied "Does a bear shit in the woods?" He was in.

Collen remembers working with Lange for the first time as a great initiation. The first time he played in the studio Lange stopped him and shook his head. Collen's timing was wrong, despite the fact that he was playing exactly the way he had been for years while with Girl. "I was still really in my infancy as a guitarist then" he says.

Lange just brought things out of me, introducing me to things like feel and timing. He's definitely been the biggest influence on my playing. With Girl, being in the studio was always more a laugh. People would come down and hang around, I'd play what I thought was good stuff but when I listen to it now realise some of it is pretty poor compared to what I was playing under Mutt. I was the sort of guitarist that would sometimes practice eight hours a day. I was getting better but in the wrong direction. Before Mutt nobody had really pointed out ways that I could improve my playing, and I also hadn't worked with anyone that I respected as much as him before."

Collen and Clark blended well both in the studio as well as socially. "Me and Steve played totally differently. His classical training still came through, whereas I'd been listening to things like Al Di Meola, stuff which involves a lot of speed picking and muting techniques. I really came in and did my own thing which fitted really well with what Willis had recorded." The band decided to keep all of the rhythm tracks that Willis had done, and Collen was more than happy with this, as he thought it was some of the best rhythm playing that he'd ever heard. He described playing solos over the tracks as inspiring. Meanwhile, Willis was in something of a state of shock. He'd always regarded Leppard as 'his band', not that he was the leader but he'd been there from day one. "I felt really strange. One minute you're in a band that are set to conquer the world and the next five years are planned for you and the next you're sitting at home twiddling your thumbs not knowing what to do. It was very disheartening."

IT'S JUST A GAME,
A GROWN UP GAME

L eppard continued recording what would become 'Pyromania' throughout 1982. On a visit to New York, Joe was introduced to his all time hero, Mott The Hoople's Ian Hunter, for the first time. They sat and chatted until four o'clock in the morning. The two have since become friends, and Joe said of that first meeting "I was so happy that you could have shot me and the bullet would have passed straight through my body. I kept thinking 'this is him, this is him!' We were chatting about things on the same level, musician to musician, yet I still felt like a little boy. I'd already met the bands that I'd got into as a teenager which is always enjoyable, especially if they turn out to be nice people, but meeting Ian Hunter for the first time was something else."

In Britain, Mensch had said that the new Def Leppard album would change the face of heavy rock. He was, of course, smiled at indulgently. He was, after all, someone who always seemed to know what would be happening, someone with his finger on the pulse. But now, like a proud father, he'd been fooled into thinking that his offspring was somehow better than all the others. Since the last album, Mensch and Burnstein had broken from Leber-Krebs and, ever the intellectuals, decided to call the new company Q-Prime. The name comes from a derivative of pure maths, or calculus. Prime denotes the rate of change of the function of Q, meaning that the Quantity of Q is dependant on the rate of change of another quantity. Mensch and Burnstein used the name to signify that the rate of change in the management company is directly related to the growth of the bands it manages. And Def Leppard were about to grow in a way that no one, not even Mensch at his most confident, could have predicted.

Lange completely revolutionised the band, and in doing so revolutionised the way rock music is recorded. He would take a chord, break it down, sample it and put it back together again. Ironically, Collen's solo on 'Stagefright', the one that got him into the band in the first place, was also the quickest thing that Lange worked on, taking him only half an hour to get the sound exactly how he wanted it. For the backbeat, Lange had used a linn drum, which is like a sophisticated drum machine and up to that point was only in use by disco and synthesiser bands like The Human League,for the basic track, the 'click track' for the band to get the rhythm right. This meant that Allen had several weeks to work out what would be the best possible drum

patterns for each song, while the band played to the machine. Lange again took the songs apart, and was credited with co-writing many of them. The version of 'Photograph' that ended up on the album contained only the bridge and chorus of the song that Leppard had originally entered the studio with. Each instrument was recorded separately, so that any single one could have been wiped and redone at any time. "It was like making a movie" Elliot said. "None of the bits are done in order, so you don't really know what you've got until you see the final thing. The way we recorded 'Pyromania' made Queen's stuff seem like a four track demo."

Towards the end of the recording, Joe had to take two weeks off to rest his throat as it had gone through so much wear and tear. There were also rumours that the singing on the album was not all Joe's own work, that Terry Wilson-Slesser, former vocalist with British band Back Street Crawler, had sung on two of the tracks. Joe was asked about this, and adopted a deadly serious expression. I'll be honest" he said ".....he sang all of them. I didn't sing on the album at all. Nah, that's just ridiculous. He was in the studio, and did do some singing, but only as part of The Leppardettes who sang backing on 'Rock Of Ages'." 'The Leppardettes' comprised of Wilson- Slesser, Manfred Mann's Chris Thomas, Rocky Newton from Leppard's old support band Lionheart and Pete 'Overend' Watts, formerly with Mott The Hoople and by then running an antique shop. The rumour regarding different singers on the album was one that was to surface from time to time, as was the one that Rick Allen hadn't played drums on the album and that the bass lines were all done by computer. "If someone says these things often enough then people start to say 'there's no smoke without fire'" said Joe a year or so after the release of 'Pyromania'. "All we can do is say they should see us do the songs live, but even then they'd probably say the whole thing was on tape."

Pyromania was released during a British tour in February 1983, and did completely shake everyone's expectations. The sleeve featured a design by the company Satori which many thought looked cheap, a drawing of a building being fired on viewed through a telescopic sight. One of the people to get thanked on the album was Steve Mann, former guitarist with Liar who had supported UFO on their 1979 tour and more recently had been a member of Lionheart. Mann, who went on years later to join The Michael Schenker Group, was surprised by this, recalling that all he'd done was lend them an amp. "I thought that if everyone who did them a favour was thanked the album would have a 'thank you' list as long as your arm" he said later. "It was nice to be thanked on one of the biggest selling albums of all time, but I wish I'd have told them to give me a penny for every copy the album sold." Joe was later to say that they put him on simply because they all thought he was a 'really nice bloke' and had come up trumps when they needed a different amp to get the right sound.

Critically, the album met with strong approval. One magazine, previously luke-warm towards Leppard, called it 'the greatest rock album since Led Zeppelin's 'Physical Graffiti'. The album was preceded by the single 'Photograph', written by Joe about Marilyn Monroe. "I saw 'Some Like It Hot' and I just thought she was the most beautiful woman in the world." The band also recorded a video for the song. Since the success of the 'Bringin' On The Heartbreak' video in America, sales of 'High'n'Dry' had trebled, and the band were hoping that a video for 'Photograph' could pave the way for a similar thing to happen to 'Pyromania'. What actually happened was nothing short of a phenomenon, 'Photograph' being immediately put on heavy rotation on MTV, and Leppard's fan base was suddenly rocketing. The combination of youth and good looks was working for them. Joe wore a Union Jack t-shirt in the video, taking the idea from the shorts that Rick had worn. Once they really took off in America, this idea would expand to merchandising Def Leppard Union Jack t-shirts, the sale of which was phenomenal. The irony was not lost on Peter Mensch. "It's funny. Def Leppard get slagged off for selling out to America, yet there's thousands upon thousands of American kids walking round in British flag t-shirts because of them."

In Britain though, Leppard were once again only playing one nighters, most of them only doing about 60% business. After a show at the Colston Hall in Bristol, Joe sat in the bar of the Dragonara Hotel sipping hot toddies to ease a painful throat further exacerbated by 'flu, and reflected on this: "I suppose it's because we seem so arrogant that people here hate us. People talk about us selling out to America and kinda, you know, why? Because we were the FIRST. We burned the trail for everyone else to follow. Maiden, Saxon, UFO, you name it have been there as much if not more than us but because we were the first to go we got burnt for it, really badly." He felt that the situation in Britain was really unfair, that Leppard had been picked on. "In my opinion you're a brave lad if you admit to liking Def Leppard. I really feel that. It's like admitting to liking Uriah Heep in 1974 when everyone was into Deep Purple. We're gonna end up losing £40,000 on this tour and the only reason we can afford to do that is because we're earning a bit of money abroad. We're still lots and lots of money in debt, but people over here never believe us, they all think we're millionaires."

He also defended his lyrics, which one critic had dismissed as 'A series of heavy metal clichés, not worthy of the music that they accompany.' "I write lyrics to fit songs. I take them seriously, but especially when they're a piss take. If I'm gonna take the piss out of something I'm gonna do it properly. The song 'Rock Of Ages' I wanted to be well over the top, 'Rock Rock' was another. That's just something to get the crowd involved, a bit of a singalong, time to clap your hands. I get really fed up writing songs with the word 'rock' in the title. 'Rocks Off', 'Rock Brigade', 'Rock 'Till You Drop' there's billions of them, but they're just for fun, the 'let your hair down, who gives a shit' songs. The serious ones are things like 'Die Hard The Hunter' which was inspired by the film 'The Deer Hunter' and 'Billy's Got A Gun' about a mixed up guy who is out to get somebody, anybody, for no particular reason. 'Action Not Words' is about picking sluts up in Soho. It was just the Indian sounding guitar on it, like a cross between Jimmy Page and George Harrison, made it sound really seedy, so the lyrics are seedy too. The lyrics poke fun but out of ourselves. I couldn't sing a line like 'Hold on hold tight we're gonna rock tonight' and really get off on them. Reading them back you think 'oh dear, that looks a bit naff' but when you hear it, it's just fun." He also revealed that Mutt's production technique had afforded them some fun. During Phil's solo in 'Rock Of Ages' there are some strangely garbled words. This is actually Joe singing the phrases 'Brezhnev's got herpes' and 'fuck the Russians.' Never one for too much political correctness, Joe was to get in trouble later in 1983 for calling El Paso, Texas "the place with all those greasy Mexicans." This resulted in a threat of disruption of a gig in El Paso on their 1988 tour, and the gig had to be cancelled. Joe also revealed that the untitled run off track after 'Billy's Got A Gun' at the end of 'Pyromania' is called 'The March Of The Dreaded Zultrons', a result of Allen messing around with the linn drum by pressing a few numbers and arriving at that rhythm, over which the band stuck some odd sounding keyboards. He also revealed that Willis had come to see the band play Sheffield and still hadn't conquered his drinking problem. The woman who ran Sheffield City Hall was about seventy years old and hated all the young rock bands who would play there, and most were scared of her. Willis arrived drunk and was unable to find his backstage pass. Walking towards the dressing room area, the woman challenged Willis as to where he was going, to which he replied "I want to go backstage you fat old bastard." It was only when one of Leppard's crew rescued him that he got to the dressing room, but not before he'd been made to apologise. The band's parents were backstage, and the sight of Willis lurching around was recalled by Joe's dad as being 'very sad to see.'

After a show at the Hammersmith Odeon (again only one night, plenty of tickets available on the door) the band held a party at the Clarendon Hotel, just over the road from the Odeon and itself a small venue where mainly punk bands played. 'Pyromania' was by now top ten in America, but Joe played down any excitement he may have felt about this, stressing disappointment at the attendances on this tour. Steve Clark said he'd enjoyed the tour, and felt it may be in some way the calm before the storm of going to America, saying that if the album continued to sell as well as it had been, and feedback from their record company didn't suggest that it wouldn't, the American tour could be 'completely crazy'.

A couple of weeks later Joe was in attendance at Frank's Funny Farm, a small cocktail bar situated under the Kypriana Hotel in Chalk Farm, North London. It had become something of a hang out for minor heavy rock stars, music business hangers on and wannabees, the owner always being (overly) friendly to anyone who was, or might seem, remotely famous and/or pretty, and for a while it became like a mini version of Los Angeles' Rainbow Bar And Grill. By now 'Pyromania' was top five in America, and Joe's attitude was very different. "Top five makes it for real. That's really big. I don't know why I feel that, but seeing our album pushing up against the biggest bands in the world is just staggering." He also agreed he may have been slightly defensive about the success of the LP during the tour. "The problem is, if I seem really excited by success in America then I'll just get hammered again, people will say that's all I care about. But now we're top five I AM really excited. People should be happy for us, happy that a British band has gone and done this, rather than slagging us off all the time. What do people want, us to be unsuccessful in America and go there like other bands, third on the bill to Yank acts? I wore the union Jack t-shirt in the 'Photograph' video and now on stage to knock it into a few people's heads that we're not selling out to America, but I'm starting to feel that I can't be bothered banging my head against a brick wall anymore. I'm fed up having to apologise for being successful in another country. People should be proud that a British band can have such big success abroad. If people still say we've sold out then bollocks to them, people with any sense at all know the truth."

After the British tour Leppard went to Europe, returning a couple of months later to play a one off gig at the Marquee. By now Leppard were solidly established as a phenomenon, and the Marquee was packed with hangers on. Since they'd been away 'Pyromania' had stayed top five, and it's success had meant a softening of attitude towards Leppard. People in Britain had started listening to the album, mainly due to it's

success in America. A typical example was an overheard conversation at the Marquee gig, where one fan was berating a journalist who'd slagged Leppard off. "I'd not bothered listening to them because of what you'd written" the fan said to the writer "But I got hold of this new album because I thought there must be something to it if so many Americans are buying it, and it's brilliant. I can't believe we have to learn about one of our own bands through their popularity in another country." It was an argument that many were to repeat over the coming months.

Also at the Marquee gig was Brian Robertson, former Thin Lizzy guitarist who was just on his way out of Motorhead. He spoke of the rumours that 'Pyromania' was just a studio album, that Leppard were Mutt Lange's pet band. He reckoned this to be pure jealousy on everyone else's part. "People can't accept that Leppard are this good, so these rumours come out, but out of all these new heavy metal bands they're the only ones with any original ideas. If Lange helped them in the studio then so what? If I could get an album sounding as good as theirs I'd sell my soul to the Devil, so a little help with arrangements is a small price to pay!"

After the gig the band held another party, this time at the newly opened Cafe Pacifico Mexican restaurant in Covent Garden. Among the people in attendance were Neil Murray, Whitesnake's bass player, and a man who was becoming a regular feature at these kind of affairs, and Phil Soussan, a friend of Joe's who would go on to play bass with, amongst others, Ozzy Osbourne. The restaurant's extensive menu in it's entirety was available, as well as all cocktails, and the record company ended up with a five figure bill. During the party Joe was asked about the forthcoming American tour. "It's a feeling of excitement and trepidation. We're going there to play to an audience that, apart from a few rock fans, only knows us from MTV. It'll be fun."

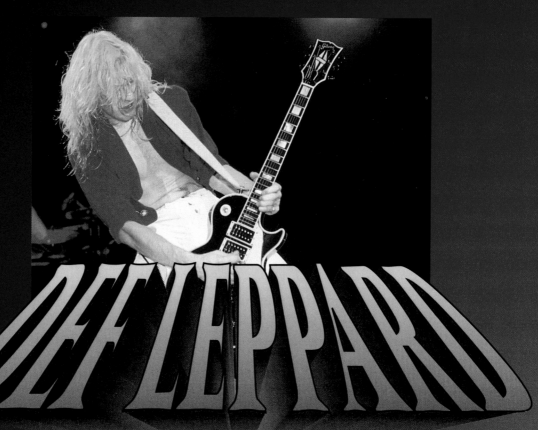

Chapter Seven

ACTION NOT WORDS

A merica was now theirs for the taking. Since the 'Photograph' video, the band had released two more songs from the album in America, and the accompanying videos which, like 'Photograph', had been directed by David Malletthad were again been shown on heavy rotation on MTV. 'Rock Of Ages' had started with an appearance by Peter Mensch uttering the 'untag leiben louten loubon' (the spelling of which has been done at least three different ways) at the beginning of the song, and featured Joe wielding a sword as the songs hero. Joe was later to say he felt like a complete prat while doing it. The line 'It's better to burn out than fade away' was marginally borrowed from Neil Young's 'Hey Hey My My', and was also borrowed by director Russell Mulcahy for his 1985 film 'Highlander'. Mulcahy incidently shared a flat with Phil Collen's ex guitar partner in Girl, Gerry Laffy.

The video to 'Foolin'' featured Billy Idol's sometime girlfriend Perri Lister, and starts with a shot of Joe that he felt showed his double chin badly. Joe and Rick Savage both suffered from weight gain when not on the road, although Joe managed to keep his in check more, Savage tending to lose pounds during a show that, during periods of inactivity, made him look slightly bloated. (Check the Def Leppard 'Rock Of Ages' video that is mentioned in the acknowledgements at the start of this book for further proof.) 'Foolin'' also featured a segment where the whole band leap backwards out of a hole and Phil and Steve turn to look at Joe. Although it's meant to be a serious moment Phil looks about twelve years old and Steve like he's just about to burst out laughing. The band were always to look odd on video when not playing their instruments, although Joe's sense of the dramatic- he really 'acts his socks off' as someone wrote at the time in the 'Foolin'' video- means he usually comes out of it OK.

In America though, the videos were seen as manna from heaven. One article at the time, a 'thinkpiece' in one of the more upmarket magazines, compared their coming to that of a new British Invasion, such as that of the Beatles. Just as The Beatles arrived at a time when America was looking for something to focus on following the assassination of John F. Kennedy the article stated 'so now Def Leppard arrive just after the passing of the last vestiges of the so-called punk era. Now that it's once again 'media acceptable' for bands to play hard rock there comes a band who have produced a totally new sound albeit within a limited field of music. They also look like a teenagers dream, all long hair and pouting lips and have already proven, on previous tours with America's own Ted Nugent and German band The Scorpions, that they have musical ability when on stage too. This could be the year that Leppard clean up.'

The band were to be supported on tour by Krokus,a blatant AC/DC rip-off band from Switzerland featuring Cypriot vocalist Marc Storace. Krokus had had minor success in America, most notably with the song 'Bedside Radio', although in Britain they were seen as 'nuggets' (the name given at the time for all the young heavy rock fans who had emerged in the early eighties with neatly pressed denim jackets and patches sewn on by their parents) band, and no self respecting rock fan would have anything to do with them. Leppard's success with the crowd was instant and phenomenal, many audiences were impressed with the sheer quality of the backing vocals, Savage's in particular. 'Although Elliot is the star of the show' ran a review of their Los Angeles gig 'and a more natural frontman it would be hard to find, you get the feeling that in another life Rick Savage would have been equally as good, oozing sex appeal and with a voice that often overshadows Elliot's basic throaty roar.'

During the tour one of the roadies noticed something strange during Krokus' set. Joe had developed set stage raps, which he justified at the time by saying that sometimes it was easy to waffle. "I have set things that I say because they work. they're just part of the set. If we finish off a song like 'Rock Of Ages' and I say 'yeah cheers, um, 'ope you're all 'avin' fun' it would sound really stupid, so I'll say something a bit more interesting than that. I say them in a dramatic voice which some people have said sounds American, but I can't help that. You try sounding dramatic with a broad Yorkshire accent." On the tour Joe had noticed that some of his raps were not having the desired effect, the crowd would not react as well as he knew they ought to.The roadie reported that Storace had been ripping off Joe's raps, and subsequently Joe was just repeating what the crowd had heard just an hour or so before. One night Joe watched from the side of the stage. "I couldn't believe it, there was this guy saying everything I was going to say, word for word. I just stood there open mouthed. No wonder the crowd looked at me like I was an idiot. It must have been like watching an action replay." Leppard confronted Krokus about this, and Krokus's manager denied it.

The atmosphere on the tour became decidedly frosty, especially once the story leaked out in the rock press. There was talk of Rick Allen being confronted with a knife one night, although this was never substantiated. Krokus' manager actually said that he'd make sure Def Leppard never worked in America again, intimating that Krokus had some connections in high places. This of course was the wrong thing to say, as a public slagging of America's current favourites was not going to win Krokus any friends.

In Britain Peter Mensch attended shows on the Rush tour. Rush were, he said, the band above all others that he'd like to manage but didn't. He chatted about Leppard's American success, something that he had predicted all along. "I said before this album came out that it would change the course of music and people thought I was bullshitting . I don't bullshit." When approached by people saying how surprised they were at Leppard success, he would almost bark that they "don't know anything about music." He also spoke of his disappointment in Iron Maiden's latest album, 'Piece Of Mind', but again sounding more like a fan than a manager. There was also talk of him taking over the career of another band who'd been associated with The New Wave Of British Heavy Metal, Diamond Head. Mensch thought Diamond Head had huge possibilities, and MCA, Diamond Head's record company at the time, were desperate to get him involved. MCA's head of A&R, Charlie Eyre, was the man who'd signed Diamond Head to the label and felt that the band's management which consisted of the singer Sean Harris' mum and her partner were way out of their depth. He saw similarities between Leppard's previous management and Diamond Head's current one, but, according to Eyre at the time, it would have been to difficult to get Diamond Head out of their management contract as Harris was happy with things the way they were. MCA were to drop Diamond Head in December 1983 due to a lack of real success, and Eyre was seemingly proved right about the band's relatively weak managerial guidance. The band split a few months later reforming in 1991 but with limited success.

Following months of American success, the band played Britain again in the December, and ticket demand was, as it should be, very strong. While they'd been away British rock fans had re-evaluated the band, and perceived their success in America as something positive. How and why this happened is down to 'Pyromania's' strength as an album, plus rock had become more mainstream, meaning that a fair percentage of the crowd didn't know or didn't care about incidents such as the Reading festival three years earlier. The crowd was also bolstered by a large percentage of Americans, and Hammersmith Odeon, where the band played for two nights and sold both of them out, reported a request for over two hundred tickets from one United States Air Base in England. For one of the nights they were joined by Queen's Brian May for an encore of the old Creedence Clearwater Revival song 'Travellin' Band', which they had started doing some months earlier. The Hammersmith shows seemed slightly flat, the band seeming tired after all the excesses of America.

While in the UK the band recorded a special one off edition of an early seventies British TV show, Supersonic, which was to be broadcast at Christmas. The show's producer Mike Mansfield was known for the spectacular effects such as moving stages and fire breathing dragons that he would use to embellish the artist's performances. Joe was excited about appearing on it as one of his hero's, Marc Bolan, had made a very memorable appearance on the show some years earlier. The band mimed to 'Too Late For Love' but in hospitality before the show they had drunk a little too much champagne with the other artists on the show, including one Elton John with whom Joe had a long and engrossing conversation about football. At the time Elton was chairman of Watford and Joe asked him about players he had met, speaking to him about the ex-Sheffield United star Tony Currie, Joe's all time favourite who had earned far fewer caps for his country than he should have. The performance, which is available on the 'Historia' commercially released video, shows the band, in particular Sav, as looking 'well refreshed'. At one stage a close up of Allen shows him looking at the camera with a confused look on his face. In true Supersonic fashion, Steve and Phil are standing on staircases which are lowered as the song progresses. As they said later, it's lucky they were miming.

The band went on to play at a two day 'Heavy Metal Festival' on Saturday and Sunday 20th & 21st December at the Westfallenhalle in Dortmund, Germany. This was to be filmed for transmission all over Europe and the line up was astonishing. Iron Maiden were to be the top of the bill (something which reflected their huge popularity in Europe, although they were not making nearly as many inroads into the American market as they wished) with Leppard, Ozzy Osbourne, Judas Priest, The Scorpions, Michael Schenker Band, Quiet Riot...and Krokus. No communication had taken place between the bands since the American Tour, but Krokus had alienated themselves from most of the other bands there with their actions; Iron Maiden's affable blonde haired guitarist Dave Murray summing up many people's feelings when he said Krokus had 'overstepped the mark.' "You don't tour with someone and then take the piss out of them. It's a bit unprofessional."

Leppard were playing the Saturday only, whereas most other bands including Maiden were to play both days. Most bands were staying in the same hotel, and the bar was a star spotters paradise. On the Friday night Phil Collen spoke excitedly of the past year."It's like the world's exploded" he reckoned. "We get out of the car or bus at a gig and there's just so many women waiting. Women actually faint when they see us. It's like being a fucking Osmond brother!"

Despite the upward spiral of success, Collen seemed not to have changed a bit since his days in Girl, even checking on whether I had a pass for the next days show (I didn't) and sorting one out before going to bed. Later that night I was chatting in a bedroom with Rick Allen and Mike McNamee, a pleasant young man who worked for Iron Maiden's merchandising company and who had helped to sort out accommodation for people (including two journalists) who had arrived in Dortmund hoping to get a hotel room but found most of them booked. A knock at the door found a young not unattractive woman there who none of us had met before. Coming in, she promptly removed most of her clothing, introduced herself as Helga and got into bed, giving Allen a look that could not possibly be misinterpreted. He just raised his eyes to the ceiling and said goodnight, leaving a very angry young woman to storm out of the room with only a sheet round her and her clothes in her hand (a sheet that McNamee was charged for, so if you're reading this Helga...).

The show itself was something of a let down, Leppard being saddled with a very poor sound. Leppard did come across Krokus, with one of Krokus's roadies shouting insults at them from outside their dressing room. He soon shifted when the door was opened, and two of the Leppard crew came striding out. Krokus were soon to disappear anyway. When asked about the incident a while later Joe recalled it as being a joke. "It was funny. Krokus were saying we'd compromised our integrity or whatever because Mutt had co-written some of the songs on 'Pyromania' and then they rip us off word for word. Who's lost integrity there?"

At the beginning of 1984 Leppard travelled to Japan for the first time for some shows and interviews. Just before they left it was announced that Joe had been voted 'Worlds Sexiest Man' in a Japanese poll, so they travelled with some confidence. On a stopover at Anchorage airport, Rick Allen threw what one observer described as a 'childish tantrum' when he found out that his mum had been checking up on him and, it seemed, did not know where he was going. At this time Allen was still given to outbursts of this sort, and an insult of Whitesnake as 'old men' earned him a ticking off from David Coverdale who in turn called Allen 'a little prick'. People tended to forget that, although he'd been famous with Def Leppard since 1979, Rick Allen was still only 20 years old. In Japan they stayed in the same hotel as ex-Rainbow singer Graham Bonnet's new band, then featuring future guitar hero and 'rocks Mr ego' as he was soon to be dubbed, Yngwie Malmsteen, current teenybop idols Duran Duran and another of Mensch's charges The Michael Schenker group. They also mimed to 'Rock Rock' for Japanese TV, although the band didn't know why they

wanted that particular song with it not being released as a single (although it was an often requested album track).

In Britain the band appeared on TV in an interview filmed while they were on tour in America, on a small cruiser at sea. The premise of the interview was really to show how the band were household names in America yet, until recently, couldn't get arrested in their own country. Joe berated the media over their then obsession with Culture Club and singer Boy George, saying that the only reason he got publicity was because he wore a dress. It was also to be one of the first times Joe spoke of how many albums they'd sold, something he was accused of doing too much over the ensuing years. Rick Allen spoke enthusiastically about staying at the Edgwater Inn in Seattle where he could fish out of the window. This was also the hotel where Led Zeppelin carried out the notorious shark incident, where a girl was allegedly rodgered with a red snapper. To some it was a measure of the bands innocence that it was the fishing they should rave about.

In February they recorded two videos in Ireland, one for a re-recorded and re-mixed 'Bringin' On The Heartbreak' and one for 'Me & My Wine', which had been the original b-side of 'Bringin' On The Heartbreak' when it was released as a single in Britain in November 1981. The videos were again to be directed by David Mallett. Bringin' On The Heartbreak' actually caused both Joe and Steve problems, as the shots of them outside- Steve for his solo, and Joe on a raft for another 'actory' bit- were done in sub zero temperature and took several hours to get right. Afterwards Joe said he was "numb for about three days." The decision to redo the song came about because Leppard felt it was 'the Def Leppard hit single that was never a hit single', but had done them so much good when first shown on MTV. Also, the first time round was only a live performance, whereas this was a full blown mini epic. 'Me And My Wine' however only took about three hours. The band had spent all of their previous tour watching videos of The Young Ones BBC television series, starring performers from The Comic Strip club in London, and had picked up mannerisms and used to re- enact scenes from the series. Although they hated the song 'Me And My Wine', which they thought was 'too basic' they thought it would be fun to use the song as the basis of a spoof Young Ones video. The song was done in a semi-detached house, with the band playing in the bathroom. Clark in particular manages to look like Rik Mayall, and could do an uncanny impersonation of his voice. Allen's drum kit features the legend 'Deaf Leopard', and Joe sings into the microphone. Joe was later to say this was his favourite Leppard video.

Earnings were now starting to come in for 'Pyromania', and the band found themselves in a punitive position tax wise. British tax laws being what they were, the band decided to relocate to Dublin with it's altogether more relaxed levels of taxation. They also liked the laid back lifestyle, and were not alone in this. Members of popular groups like the Thomson Twins and Spandau Ballet had also relocated there. It was on relocation that Phil Collen decided to give up alcohol. One afternoon in Grafton Street, Dublin's well known shopping area, he'd bought a Rolex wristwatch for £6,000 while "completely bolloxed". He decided soon after this that enough was enough. With at least one member having a clearer head, Leppard set about writing material for a follow up to 'Pyromania'.

In August 1984 the band entered Wisseloord Studios in Hilversum, Holland to record a follow up to 'Pyromania.' This time they had chosen to work with Jim Steinman, best known for his production on Meat Loaf's 'Bat Out Of Hell' album. They'd chosen him as Lange was unavailable, working on the Cars album 'Heartbeat City.' The band didn't hit it off with Steinman at all, nor he with them. He complained that they didn't have a clue what each one of them had played on 'Pyromania', this being due to Lange's way of putting each instrument down separately. "It was pretty obvious from the start that Steinman was wrong" recalled Phil Collen. "It had seemed like a good idea because in some ways we were worried about making another 'Pyromania', just repeating a successful formula." Steinman has since said the sessions were 'a nightmare.' The band had got used to Lange's way of doing things, and whereas they would work with him towards a finished project, or one idea might spark several more, they felt there was no such communication with Steinman. "We like to do everything very precisely" says Collen. "He seemed to want to get us in a room and for us to play live, but that wasn't how we did things. I have a whole tape reel to record my guitars on, I do 32 tracks and then dub them down. He wanted us to do it his way. It was as if we were recording a Jim Steinman album, not him recording a Def Leppard album."

The band remember that Steinman seemed to hardly be in the studio, and whereas Lange had become almost the sixth member of the band they now felt they had a producer they were having to fight every step of the way. After three months, in November, they fired him. "The stuff he came up with just wasn't us" said Joe. "Looking back, Steinman was about as much good to us as a chocolate fireguard". Steinman himself said that there was a 'lack of intelligence' in the band. "I remember when I went to Dublin with them, I said how nice it was to be in the city of Yeats and Joyce, and Joe Elliot said they hadn't had the chance to meet any local musicians yet...."

The band had to scrap three months of expensive recording, studio time costing them around £1,000 per day. The band then decided to work with Nigel Green, Lange's engineer who had been assistant engineer on 'High'n'Dry'. They figured at the time that having someone who knew the way they recorded, plus was going to be on their side, would give them the push they needed to come up with material. They took a break for Christmas, but 1985 was going to be a fresh start. When asked by a European magazine for his Christmas hopes, Joe said that he wanted to have a new album in the shops for people to buy the following Christmas, and that the frustrations of the last few months recording would turn out to be positive signs for the future. On the music front at least, he was to be proved right. Eventually.

THE WORST THING THAT COULD HAPPEN TO A BAND

O n the afternoon of New Years Eve 1984 Rick Allen had just taken his Dutch girlfriend Miriam Barendsen to the Ladybower reservoir near Sheffield, one of the local beauty spots and was on his way to his parents house. He was travelling down the A57 Manchester Road towards Sheffield when an Alfa Romeo came screaming up near him as if to challenge him. Rick was driving a new Corvette Stingray, and this was why the Alfa driver wanted to burn him up. He thought nothing of it but the Alfa slowed down and wouldn't let him pass. Rick was getting frustrated, knowing that the Stingray could take the Alfa in a race but not wanting to enter into a contest. This continued for about four miles, by which time he'd had enough, and put his foot down on the accelerator, leaving the Alfa standing. Being a left hand drive car Rick hadn't seen a left hand turn until it was to late. The car hit a wall on the curve and flipped over. Rick shot through the windscreen, his left arm being completely severed by his seat-belt. Miriam was badly bruised. Both were taken to The Royal Hallamshire Hospital in Sheffield where Rick had four hours of micro-surgery to sew his arm back on. It also looked as if he may lose his right arm as well, due to it being so badly damaged when he landed.

The rest of the band were in deep shock. Joe recalled how he sat and cried until he could cry no more. The micro-surgery failed to save Rick's left arm when infection set in after three days, and it had to be amputated. The only positive thing at the time seemed to be that at least he was still alive, although he was to say later that there were times when he wished he wasn't. His life was only saved because he had remained conscious throughout the crash. After three days it looked like his right arm would be OK, but Allen was completely down, certain that he wouldn't be able to drum again. The Hospital reported that they'd received hundreds of cards, many from America where the crash made headline news, with Rick's progress being reported on news bulletins on a regular basis. Everyone who went and saw him reported how down he was, they tried to cheer him up, to tell him his career wasn't over but, as Joe said, "who ever heard of a one armed drummer?" There had been one, in a long forgotten early '70's band, but they were not top class. Def Leppard could hardly continue with someone who wasn't up to the task, but it was Mutt Lange, and encouragement from Peter Mensch, who actually got Rick thinking that maybe he could play the drums at the top level again.

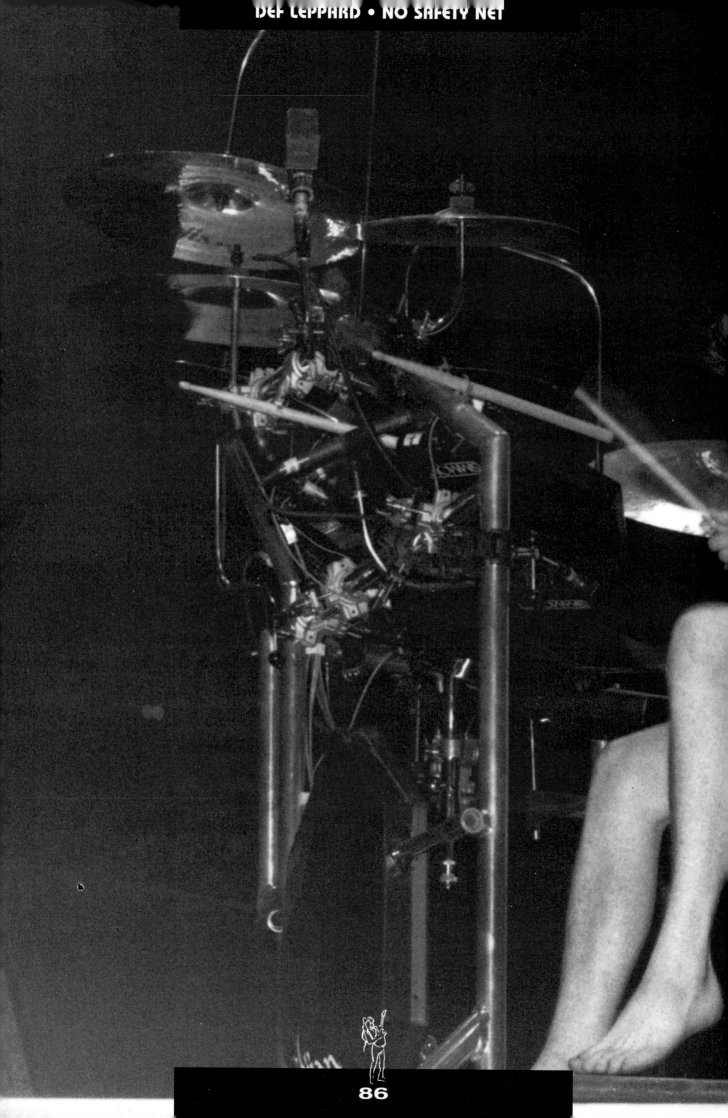

Def Leppard were already behind schedule with their new album, and needed to get recording quickly. That they were prepared to wait for Allen, to see whether he felt capable of re-learning the drums, says more for the character of the band than anything. They left it entirely up to him, and had the backing of their record company and management in this. While lying in his hospital bed, Allen had started tentatively working out rhythm patterns using his left foot where he used to us his left arm. He'd never played with a double bass drum so beloved of hard rock drummers, so his right foot was the only one for the beat, while his left he used for the hi-hat. A local firm made him some pedals and he would practice with these for hours. The band noticed a change every time they saw him, as he worked out more and more drum patterns. He discharged himself from hospital early, but not before he'd had to re-learn to walk. "The first time I tried to walk I flew across the room and hit a wall" he said. "Your balance completely goes, and the weight of the right arm needed to be compensated for."

He contacted Ian Croft who worked for the drum company Zildjian, who set about helping him design a new kit. The band meanwhile had returned to Holland. They would once again be using a click track for the drums as on 'Pyromania' but whereas then it was so Rick could do the best drum parts possible, now it was a necessity. At the time Joe said he wasn't really sure whether Rick could re-join the band, at least not on his own. They decided to look at the prospect of another drummer playing alongside Rick, and settled on Jeff Rich of Status Quo. Things had also not gone to plan with Nigel Green.

In June, Lange was played some of the songs the band had come up with, and was not impressed. He just heard a clone of 'Pyromania', and felt the band were not loosening up enough. "It was as if they were getting scared of failure, and were constricting themselves to what they already knew. I'd always got them to restructure the way they wrote songs, but it seemed like they'd either lost the ability to do that or weren't opening themselves up enough. 'Pyromania' was such a huge album that they really needed something different to make the follow up successful." The band decided to wait until Lange was once again able to be installed in the producers chair and they decided to scrap everything they'd recorded up to that time. This was to be a total of one year and four months of work.

During a short break in England, and on his birthday on August 1st 1985, Joe went to see one of his heroes Mick Ronson, who was sadly to die of cancer at the end of 1993. Ronson had played firstly with David Bowie in The Spiders From Mars, and later with Ian Hunter. The gig was at the Fulham Greyhound pub in West London, and it was one of the first times Joe had been seen at a gig for quite a while. He spoke of the year so far, and of his disappointment in Steinman. He was cagey about the news of a new drummer, even though that week The Sun (British daily tabloid at the very bottom end of the gutter press market) had published an 'exclusive' story stating that Rich was the new Def Leppard drummer for the purpose of live work, although he would be playing along with Allen. Joe revealed that Allen had a customised Simmons drum kit built, using electronic pads rather than conventional drums, and was working out the drum parts on his own with the aid of a Fairlight computer. He even managed to laugh about the situation that the band found themselves in. "We recorded an album that sold millions of copies, and here I am two years later a nobody. It's like Ian Paice (Deep Purple and Whitesnake drummer) said after Purple first split up, 'I used to be Ian Paice you know.' I was in a restaurant the other night and someone asked if I was in a band. I told them I used to be Joe Elliot out of Def Leppard!" He also talked about the Live Aid concert that had taken place a couple of weeks previously in London and Philadelphia, and of the reformation of Led Zeppelin for it. "There was one brilliant moment where Plant looks at Page while he's playing the guitar and gives him a wry smile, like after all the bollocks that's gone on between them they are still Page and Plant, probably the ultimate rock song writers ever." The gig saw Ronson accompanied by a female pianist and was disappointing. Afterwards Joe went for a birthday meal with a party that included Rush bassist Geddy Lee.

Chapter Nine

RECORD . . .
AND RECORD . . .
AND RECORD

D
ef Leppard were to take nearly two years of recording the follow up to 'Pyromania' with Lange, and Joe's 'I used to be' story was starting to ring true. They even had some t-shirts made up in response to questions about the new album, which bore the legend 'Don't ask....if it was finished you would have heard it.' During this period they'd decided to play a few warm up shows, with both Rick and Jeff Rich on the drums, and the band started live rehearsals at Studio Des Dames in Paris/ They'd also received an invitation to play the following year's 'Monsters Of Rock' festival, including the British one which had taken place every year since 1980 and was now established as the most important day of the rock calender. During one of the warm up shows, at Ballybunion in Eire, Rich was forty minutes late, and Rick had to play on his own. This worked, and so it was agreed that, since nobody had missed Rich, Rick should carry on on his own. At the time Rick said that had he thought about it, this would have made him very nervous, but the decision was thrust upon him. "I was still nervous about going out and seeing people that I didn't know, scared that they might stare. I used to sit in and read all the time."

Leppard decided to take up the invitation to play the Monsters Of Rock festivals. Prior to their appearance at the British one on August 16th, Phonogram ran a full page advert in the music press saying 'they're back. Simply the greatest rock band in the world.' This again harked back to the days of arrogance, and one or two long time fans raised their eyebrows when they saw the ad. On the day Leppard were third on the bill, sandwiched between Motorhead and The Scorpions. The weather was appalling, so was the sound and the band were a big disappointment. One review called them 'thoroughly average', and questioned whether they were a band worth seeing live at all due to the quality of their recorded product. Joe wore red trousers, the same sort that he'd worn at Reading all those years ago, and one of the reasons that he in particular had come in for so much stick, but no one said a word. He also wore a t-shirt that was a re-print of a copy of 'The Sun' from a few months previously, with the slogan 'Freddie Starr ate my hamster'. They previewed two songs from the forthcoming album, 'Love and Affection' and 'Run Riot', which would turn out to be two of the weaker songs from the album. The one real plus point, apart from the pleasure of seeing them on stage again, was

the reception afforded to Rick Allen. Joe introduced him as 'a mate of mine, Rick Allen' and the whole crowd went mad. Allen said afterwards that he'd burst into tears at the reaction, which he described as 'unbelievable.' The band also played snippets of 'Radar Love', 'Not Fade Away' and 'My Generation' during 'Rock Of Ages', but this sounded clumsy. The feeling after the Leppard set among the crowd, the record company/ press/ hangers-on backstage, was mainly that they'd been ordinary. Many justified this by saying that they must be rusty after so long away from live work.

They returned to the recording studio after further 'Monsters Of Rock' festivals, including a final one in Mannheim, Germany, that was to be the largest audience they'd played to so far in Europe. There was also 40 key personnel from Phonogram who had come to see the band. On the day the weather was atrocious, and the band were to use a picture of this on the inner sleeve to the new album. In 1986, Def Leppard were to play a total of just nine gigs. In October of 1986, Bon Jovi released 'Slippery When Wet' an album that would go on to sell over 12 million copies worldwide, and it was an album that many felt owed a huge debt to 'Pyromania.' Leppard themselves were amazed at some of the similarities, but by now they were feeling quietly confident that their next album would again take them in a different direction.

During the recording of what would become 'Hysteria', Lange had to take time off when he nearly wrecked his leg in a car crash, and Joe contracted mumps. In July of 1987, four and a half years after they had released their last album, Def Leppard finally released something. In Britain, 'Animal' was released as a single, but in America they released 'Woman'. This was due to the fact that in Britain the band had not crossed over to non rock fans, so 'Animal' was seen as the natural choice as the first single from the album. And as Joe said at the time, "At one stage our credibility was so low in Britain we could release a single of us farting and still not sink that low again." 'Animal' got to number 6 in the UK single charts, which made it their most popular single to date.

In America though it was a different story. The band were very aware that they may lose their hardcore fans if they put out such an obvious single first. What worried them was that they could end up with a 95% female and pop audience, fans who wouldn't be there as fans unless another hit single was forthcoming. They knew that 'Woman' would not get played on the top 40 stations, but would get played on stations that real rock fans listen to; FM and AOR stations. The plan worked to perfection. Upon it's release, in August, Hysteria sold one and a half million copies in America, almost all, as far as they heard from record stores, to rock fans. The cover was once again designed by Satori, and again featured a telescopic sight. Many people were confused as to whether the illustration was a man or a dog, and in interviews around that time the band were deliberately cagey. "You take it for what you want" said Collen, "we think the meaning's clear but it's up to you to work it out."

BACK IN THE SADDLE

Hysteria' had apparently cost in the region of £7,000 per week to record, an amount that was starting to concern the ever supportive Phonogram. One employee was quoted as saying that about halfway through the recording a costing meeting within the company took place. 'when it came to the new Leppard album" he recalls "we discussed the on-going situation for about half an hour before someone just tore the figures up. It was becoming pointless to try and pin them down, and to be honest after 'Pyromania' we decided not to try."

Phonogram were to be proved right with their confidence in the band's ability to deliver. The album continued to sell and sell, mainly on the back of cleverly planned single releases. In America 'Animal', the video of which was shot in a circus and which the band thought would go top five, only ever got to number nineteen. But the climb up the charts took twelve weeks, by which time the album had sold another one and a half million copies. Right at the beginning of 1988, on January the sixth to be precise, they released the title track. This went top ten. They then became the first ever band to be presented with back to back septuple albums, for 'Pyromania' and 'Hysteria'. The world fell in love with them all over again. They had, spectacularly, rewritten for the second time the way heavy rock music would sound for the next few years.

They even found time to criticise the album, Collen stating how unhappy he was with the sound of both 'Run Riot' and 'Don't Shoot Shotgun', reckoning them to sound weak. "I'd originally envisaged them sounding like AC/DC songs" he said. "I thought they were far too polished." As a criticism, it was probably the only one the album's production received. In Japan, it won a 'best production' award from a national television show, nothing special until you realise that the award was held yearly but this was for the best production EVER, and 'Hysteria' had knocked Led Zeppelin's 'Physical Graffiti' from the top spot it had held since the awards started.

With a revolutionary album, they decided to make the ensuing tour different as well. They had decided to play in the round, meaning that the stage is positioned in the middle of the arena, and not at one end. No other rock band had ever done this, although The Police had pioneered its use in many rock venues on their 1983 'Synchronicity' tour. The idea came from Peter Mensch. The thinking behind it was that, although initially the cost would be huge, the band would actually make more money, as they would be able to utilise more seats and also the view would be greatly improved.'Rather than one front row" Mensch said "you've got four."

DEF LEPPA

Unfortunately, they couldn't bring this set to Britain, as the staging was deemed to be too large and heavy for any venues they would be playing, which at this time was to include London's Wembley Arena. The 'In The Round' tour was a spectacular success, the highlight of each evening being the introduction of Rick Allen by Joe in a mock showbiz style saying that "The best thing that ever happened to this band was...." and here he'd usually pause for corny, dramatic effect..."THE RETURN OF THE THUNDERGOD", the last three syllables lasting anything up to ten seconds. The crowd went mad every night, and it seemed that Joe had, after being criticised so often for trying to sound American, gone so over the top that no one could fail to see the joke.

Chapter Eleven
START OF THE BREAKDOWN

For the entire duration of the tour, Joe didn't touch a drop of alcohol. Unfortunately Steve Clark was going the other way, and the band were finding it more and more difficult for them to deal with. The night before the tour started, nerves had taken Clark over, and he was screaming that he didn't want to play. He started throwing himself against the wall, deliberately trying to break his hands, while a roadie was desperately trying to restrain him. Joe used to be in the room next to him on the road, but asked tour manager Ian Jeffery, who had also worked with AC/DC, to move him because of the severity of Clark's arguments on the phone with his girlfriend. It was also Joe who had to deal with Clark just before they went on stage. To keep the crowd in suspense right until the last possible moment, the band were pushed out to the 'in the round' stage in huge laundry type baskets. Steve and Joe would share one of these, as Clark couldn't be left on his own in one. He'd kick and scream trying to get out, while Joe would try and calm him down. "Sometimes it worked, but there I was night after night just about to sing in front of a huge crowd and quite honestly I felt shattered before I got on stage."

During the tour, before a gig in Wisconsin in July 1988, tragedy was once again to hit the band when crew member Steve Caytor died on stage from a brain haemorrhage. During the tour the band also heard that the master tape for 'Rocket,' which had been on board the plane bound for America which exploded over Lockerbie in England, was found fully six months after the disaster, buried in the side of a building half a mile away from the crash site.

After completing the tour in October 1988, the last gig being at the 15,000 capacity Seattle Memorial Arena, Def Leppard returned to the recording studio. Mutt Lange was unavailabe to produce the sessions, as he was working with Bryan Adams on tracks that would eventually become 'Waking Up The Neighbours', and so Leppard decided to produce themselves, working with Mike Shipley, who had engineered and mixed the band's previous three albums. They started the ball rolling with four months of recording at Studio 150 in Amsterdam.

In January of '89 the first single from these sessions, 'Rocket', was finally released in Britain, the b-side being a version of the old Engelbert Humperdink song 'Release Me' sung by the band's tour manager Melvin Mortimer, whose

brother, incidentally, had sung in the mid '70's Welsh group Racing Cars, masquerading under the single entendre name of Stumpus Maximus. In February they also played at the Brits Awards at the Royal Albert Hall in London, an awards ceremony that has since gone down as one of the worst in living memory. The Presenters were Samantha Fox, who at the time was launching a career as a singer, and Fleetwood Mac's Mick Fleetwood. The whole thing was a travesty, cues being read at the wrong time, artists coming on stage when others should have been appearing (at one stage the Four Tops were meant to appear but Joe's old nemesis Boy George came on stage instead, ad libbing "I'm the One Top") and general chaos. What made it worse was the fact that the whole thing was broadcast live on British television, ensuring that this was the first and last time this was ever done, in subsequent years the shows have been recorded and shown the following day.

The general consensus was that Leppard had come out of it OK, although in the Royal Albert Hall at the time they had sounded very quiet. Afterwards the band attended the post show celebrations at the Grosvenor House Hotel, having to endure a tantrum in the foyer when Womack & Womack arrived only to be told that they could not bring all of their children in. Working for the company that helped with ticketing the event, I was attending dressed in an ill fitting dinner jacket. Having not seen any of the members of the since before the release of 'Hysteria', and with the hectic schedule of meeting, greeting and touring that the band had been on, I was confident of not being remembered. But no. Within seconds of entering Joe had spotted me, much to my embarrassment, and came over saying "wait till I tell my mates what I saw you wearing." He chatted about the Hysteria tour and about football, having attended the Tottenham v Charlton Athletic 1-1 draw the previous Saturday with Spandau Ballet's Martin and Gary Kemp, whom he knew from his self imposed exile in Ireland. The band also attended another awards ceremony at this time, the MTV awards in Los Angeles.

They continued with writing and recording throughout 1989, and released a live video, mainly shot in Denver during February '88, of the 'Hysteria' tour, titled 'In The Round...In Your Face.' Directed by Wayne Isham, the hand picked camera crew had previously worked on major Hollywood films such as 'Platoon' and 'Apocolype Now'. During a break in activities, Phil Collen flew to Australia to produce an album by BB Steal with engineer Pete Woodroffe. BB Steal were fronted by Craig Csongrady, a longtime friend of Collen's. The LP was called 'On The Edge', and Collen produced while Woodruffe helped to engineer and mix the album.

The results meant that BB Steal ended up sounding like a poor mans Leppard, although the production was spot on, the songs didn't have the strength to take them out of the area of run of the mill rock songs. Phil's wife Jacki also gave birth to a son, Rory James, on 9th January 1990. Phil took three months off to be with his family, and it was during this time that Joe laid down most of his vocals for the album. When Phil returned, Joe took a holiday in Lanzarote. Phil reckons this gave them space to be objective about the other's work."If you're all standing round, it can sometimes be difficult to point out things that you think are wrong, or even to get a clear perspective on it. When someone's not even in the same country you tend to find it easier!"

Peter Mensch made an appearance on British television, in a segment featuring rock managers (Mensch was by now also in charge of Tesla, Metallica, Dokken and Queensryche). He said that he always tried to give his bands their independence, and that his greatest fear was that one day in the future a member of a band that he had managed would knock at his door and say 'I know we split up years ago but...I don't know what to do any more'. Also featured on the show were Dire Strait's Ed Bicknell and Led Zeppelin's legendary Peter Grant. A review of the show compared Grant and Mensch, and stated that it was interesting to note the shift in the way they managed their bands. 'Where Peter Grant would shout and scream, threatening to hurt people physically if he didn't get his way, Peter Mensch comes across as knowing what he wants and the best, most efficient way to get it. Grant completely changed the way that bands toured, asking for, and getting more of the money taken at each show than any band before. He stopped rock bands being treated like circus acts, whereby even the biggest of artists would appear on a five band bill. Mensch's sense of good business has put him on a par with Grant, but Grant's methods, although probably necessary at the time, would not work now.'

All this time the band were getting more concerned about Steve Clark. The problems that occurred on the road during the 'Hysteria' tour were getting worse. At least when on the road Clark had a routine, like he had to be on stage at 9 so he liked to be out of the shower at 8, but now that that was gone he was drinking to fill in his time. Before the band started recording a follow up to 'Hysteria', he was checked into rehabilitation five times. Each time he would leave and go round the corner to the pub. Joe subsequently stated that Steve would have been an alcoholic whether or not the band had been successful. "He was an alcoholic when he was 18, working in a factory in Sheffield. He was an alcoholic all the time we were successful. He was not a happy man. Steve Clark was the best kept secret in the world."

The band continued recording at Joe's home studio in Dublin which was equipped with an Amek 32 track desk and Mitsubishi digital. Looking back at 'Hysteria', they felt there was still some sounds that they could improve on, Collen's previous criticisms of 'Run Riot' and 'Don't Shoot Shotgun' having been noted by the rest of the band. They decided this time that they wanted to record something with more punch. The band were also recording without Clark. "He couldn't get it together any more" said Joe. "While we were in Dublin he stayed in America, we wanted him to sort himself out and get well, but we wanted to carry on recording." It seemed that Clark had only two interests in life, playing the guitar and drinking, and he had just lost interest in the guitar. "Not only could he no longer play the guitar " Joe recalled, " He no longer wanted to. While we were recording we heard that he'd been found in a gutter in Minneapolis, face down in a gutter, and taken to hospital where it was discovered that the level of alcohol in his blood was .59. This didn't really mean anything to us 'till we discovered that .41 had killed John Bonham and .30 puts most people into a coma. Steve had gone double coma and somehow still lived."

In Minneapolis, he was put into a psychiatric ward, where Joe, Rick Savage, Cliff Burnstein and 'Mutt' Lange went to see him. The four of them met Steve's doctor the night before, who asked them to write letters to Steve and read them out to him the next morning. They were told to write anything they wanted, to call him all the names under sun if they felt like it, as long as Clark realised that what he was doing was having such a bad effect on the rest of them. Joe: "We read the letters out to him and he didn't say anything, just sat with his head bowed. Some of the things we wrote were fairly strong, but we were angry with him for doing this to himself. Then he burst into tears and started telling us how sorry he was, that he didn't realise everybody cared so much." The doctors at the hospital had tried this method many times before, and it's standard practice with alcoholics. "But once he started apologising we felt sorry for him, and as soon as he saw us feel sorry for him he became arrogant."

Steve travelled back to London, where he went into rehabilitation. On more than one occasion he would stay sober for a month, and then check out and go straight to the pub. He travelled over to Dublin to try and get things together with the rest of the band, things didn't improve and he ended up in rehabilitation again. While in Dublin the doctor who was treating him asked for a family member to come so that Steve could have a 'famerial treatment' which is where a member of the addicts family-and it can be any addiction, not necessarily alcohol- will, in front of the families of other addicts, embarrass the person into both admitting their addiction, and telling the others the way this person behaves, how they spend all their money on the addiction, how upset it makes them etc etc. Steve begged Joe not to tell his parents, something Joe thought about and then, to his regret, agreed with. Peter Mensch asked Joe to go in place of Steve's family and, although he really didn't want to, he eventually agreed. He went every Wednesday for a month, and hated every minute of it. That he did speaks volumes for the character of the band. Many members of addicts families are reluctant to do it, and Joe recalls feeling really odd that here he was doing it to a fellow band member, digging out really embarrassing things about them. While he was there, talking at him, Clark would sit and stare at the floor, picking his nails like he really didn't care. For years Clark had been a 'rock star', and part of the problem was that no one had spoken to him like this all his adult life. After everyone else had left, Steve would tell Joe he really appreciated him doing it, but Joe felt this wasn't ever quite true.

In September of 1990 the band felt that Steve had changed completely, that something drastic had to be done. He was lying to them, telling them he was being weaned off drink by tablets he'd been taking, yet he'd be washing them down with alcohol. The band gave him a six month leave of absence. They didn't fire him. Phil had up to then played all of the guitar parts on the album, and was happy to carry on doing so. They told him to go home to the house he'd bought in Chelsea, London, write some songs on a demo studio he had in the basement of the house, and try and get some routine back in his life. Come February of 1991, they would see how things were. If he had gone back to them still in the same state, then they would have to consider getting someone else in the band.

FOOLIN' NO ONE

The recording continued apace. Lange had co-written many of the songs with Leppard, but all during the recording he was still working on Bryan Adams' album. Adams would later recall how the phone would ring and it would be one of Leppard, asking Mutt for his opinion while they played a bit of music down the phone to him. "We'd play pieces and Mutt would say 'yeah that sounds fine' or 'are you sure about that ending?" recalls Joe. "He wasn't there at all when we were recording, but we did get him to sing some backing vocals for us, which he'd always done, plus he's good fun to have in the studio. When there's five or six of you round a microphone there's always someone who decides to drop their trousers, and this was Mutt on more than one occasion. I know how childish that sounds but when you're recording a major album it's sometimes nice to have silly diversions." The band were actually getting the guitar parts done quicker with only Phil doing them. They used to orchestrate the parts together, but now Phil would sit and work out what Steve would have played, but quicker than Steve would have done. Joe put this down to the fact that Collen not only didn't drink, he was also a vegan and didn't smoke, meaning his mind was focussed all the time. "Steve always had distractions" he said. To get the kind of sound the band were looking for Collen would record his part three times, then layer each one. The band stayed in contact with Clark through mutual friends, not wanting to call him too much in case he thought they were checking up on him.

The reports that were filtering through were not good, and on more than one occasion Clark was seen drinking in various pubs around Chelsea, looking absolutely terrible. He was not to see out his six month leave of absence.

On the morning of 9th January 1991 he was found dead by his girlfriend in his house in Chelsea. When Joe found out, via a phone call from Cliff Burnstein, he wasn't surprised. Steve, in the classic alcoholics fashion, had lied to everyone, but mainly to himself. Alcoholics will only get better once they realise that they have a problem, and Steve never really admitted to himself that he had such an acute one. "I wasn't shocked" Joe recalled. "I was upset, but in the same way as you are when your 99 year old granny dies. I was upset, but I didn't cry. I don't know why not, perhaps it's because of all the torment we'd already been through had built up a kind of barrier. I was almost already mentally prepared for it. I felt as if the guy I knew didn't really exist anymore. When Rick lost his arm that was different, that was out of the blue, but with Steve we could see it coming for some time."

Steve's dad, Barry Clark, had always said he didn't think his
son would live until he was 30. He made it by six months.
The news shocked many people, but music industry insiders
were not surprised.There had been several reports over the
previous few months of Steve's problems, and how he was
trying to fight them. One record company employee heard
the headline 'rock guitarist dies' and immediately knew it
would be Steve. Elsewhere, in a German magazine, one
report said that it was Collen who was dead, this apparent
mix up coming about because of a confused news report that
the 'blond haired guitarist in Def Leppard' had died, and the
magazine's picture library chose a picture of Collen.

The coroner's report dated 27th February gave the cause of
Clark's death as 'respiratory failure due to an excess of
alcohol mixed with anti-depressants and painkillers.' His
blood was also found to contain traces of valium and
morphine. The day after the funeral, Leppard returned to the
studio. They were determined to carry on working, and
didn't really want to sit around until they felt like recording.
As with Rick's accident, they felt the sooner they got on
with things the better, and they also felt that Steve would
have wanted them to continue as soon as possible. They
carried on recording 'til the end of March, but realised that
nothing that they were recording sounded very good. Joe in
particular felt that his vocals sounded as though he was
reading from a card, not coming through in his usual
emotive way. They continued recording until the end of
March, but Savage recalls that none of it seemed real. "We
knew we had an album to do, and also that we couldn't give
up for Steve's sake or for our own; but suddenly for the first
time, certainly for me, it felt like we were going through the
motions."

They decided, not for the first time, to scrap what they had
recorded. Joe felt the first three months recording had
strengthened the band, that recording throughout that time
was almost like a form of mourning, but they now realised
they had to get on with their lives as Def Leppard. Once they
had realised this, what was to become 'Adrenalize' was, by
Leppard's exacting standards, recorded at lightning speed.
Rumours continued that Leppard were to break up, that
Steve's death was to be the final straw, but inside the band
there was never any thought of this.

They felt that not only would Steve have wanted them to
carry on- he'd hardly been around for such a long time
anyway- but that the material was just to good to let drop.
"Some people said that maybe we were a bit callous" says
Joe "but we were just being realists. What else would we do
anyway? This is all we've ever done, all we've ever wanted to
do. You have a period of mourning, but we didn't think it fair

to us, the fans or Steve's memory if that period went on forever, which is what it would have been if Def Leppard had ceased to exist. During this low point, the band received a boost in that the Video for 'Pour Some Sugar On Me' from 'Hysteria" had been voted number one video of all time by MTV viewers. That song also received the somewhat lesser accolade of being covered by the corny all male dance troupe 'The Chippendales'.

DEF LEPPARD

During the recording of the album, Phil Collen, bereft of a guitar partner, asked Queen's Brian May for some advice on the recording of multi track guitar and vocals that both Queen and Leppard have in common. Even then one or two rumours came out that May was actually playing on the album, even though Collen later said that the main reason he spoke to May was for advice on live work rather than recording. Leppard, it seemed, had become a band that rumours would attach themselves to. Regarding a replacement for Clark, the gossips were just about to have a field day. After the recording of the album, Joe, Sav and Phil had some light relief when, just before Christmas 1991 they participated in the Irish 'Christmas Rocks' charity gig as 'Glam Slam' performing T.Rex, Mott, Bowie and Sweet classics backed by various musical friends from the locality including Maria Doyle from the cast of the film 'The Commitments'. Further to this, Joe was seen performing on British television with Liam O'Maonlai from Irish group Hothouse Flowers, both with acoustic guitars and no backing. O'Maonlai was later to remark that Joe had a sense of musical history that he wouldn't have believed possible for someone who performs "the music that Def Leppard do."

MY EVER CHANGING MOODS

M arch 1992 saw the first new music that the band had released since December 1987 with the release of the single 'Let's Get Rocked.' This was to show the way that Leppard's sound had changed, an almost 'dancey' beat but still underlayed by the same signature Def Leppard guitar sound. Joe reckoned it to be a '90's answer to the Kiss song 'Rock'n'Roll All Night', and it originally came from a drum pattern that the band got from listening to LL Cool J. They wanted something that would sound like a Def Leppard song but also be tongue in cheek. At one stage in the song there is a sample of Mozart, plus the noise of a car. Joe had gone away for the weekend so the rest of the band went to his house and miked up a car, and then they proceeded to tear around and around his driveway in it. They were just thinking of anything that would be fun for them to record, little things that, as usual, you wouldn't quite know are there until they're pointed out to you. The solo from the song was inspired by Lange who, on hearing the basic song and what the band were trying to achieve with it, told Phil to play whatever came into his head, to forget any structure to his playing. As Collen said, everything on the song became exaggerated to the point that the solo, which would have sounded out of place on almost any other track, fitted perfectly. The song also featured some deliberately corny lyrics, the most punsome of which was the now infamous line "I suppose a rock's out of the question?' There was even a dance remix of the song, done without the band's permission, by 'DJ Coggy Dog', although this was only aired in clubs and never released commercially.

The single was a hit around the world, reaching number 2 in Britain and only missing out on being number one by 146 copies. The video that accompanied the song was fabulously expensive, an animated fantasy directed by Steve Baron who had previously directed both A-Ha's 'Take On Me' video and Dire Straits 'Money For Nothing', (both of which were ground-breaking videos for animation, based on the cult cartoon show 'The Simpsons'). The single seemed to point the way for a fresh direction for Leppard's sound, still unmistakably them but with more modern influences creeping in. Unfortunately, the album didn't live up to this promise, although the material was as strong as anything to date. Leppard almost had too much to live up to. Once again they'd had a long lay off between releases, this one longer than any previous break. Also, the musical climate was changing, but not in their favour.

Whereas their initial emergence had coincided with the death of punk and resurgence of hard rock. 'Adrenalize' was released at a time when Nirvana's 'Nevermind' album was pushing down the barriers between rock, thrash and punk. All of a sudden, the 'old crowd' were beefing up their sound, all talking about being more 'earthy'. In interviews at the time, Collen said that the new album would be rawer than any before. There was a difference in the sound, but this was mainly due to the absence of Mutt Lange. Although it had seemed for a while he would work with them as producer, the band decided that they didn't want to wait around yet another year for him, which is what would have happened because of his commitment to Bryan Adams and his 'Waking Up The Neighbours' album. The Leps decided on long time cohort Mike Shipley as the producer, although Lange got an 'executive producer' credit on the album and co-wrote most of the songs on the album. " I felt like a 'telephone producer'" he said later. "I'd be in the studio with Bryan and the phone would ring and it was Leppard saying 'listen to this, what do you think'? and I'd say yeah it sounds good or 'are you sure about the ending' and they'd go away and work on it a bit more before phoning back.' It was good that I was working with Bryan 'cos he just found it funny." Adams recalled that sometimes he'd listen as well. "A couple of times I was even tempted to borrow stuff. It was kind of odd at first the way they rang him all the time, but I got used to it."

Oddly enough the 'Waking Up The Neighbours' disc which resurrected his career and gave him a worldwide number one with 'Everything I Do (I Do It For You)', was said by many to be Def Leppard soundalike album, prompting more than one reviewer to expound the theory that, whoever you are , if Mutt produces you you're going to end up releasing a Mutt Lange album. 'Adrenalize' was released at the beginning of April, and featured the cleverest cover yet. The band wanted something to capture the feeling that the word 'Adrenalize' gave them. After several suggestions it was decided that the band would go with the blue concept cover featuring the image of an eye, the thinking behind it being another pun of adrenal...eyes. Although thought to be a computer image, the photo is that of a real eye, the eye in question belonging to model Miles Kendrick. The photo was produced with his eyelids being sellotaped apart and his head being stuck fast to a serving hatch with packing tape. He also had the arduous task of not blinking for ages while the photograph was taken. The band were very keen on this cover concept, not least for the huge marketing potential such a strong image would give them. The photography on the back cover was taken by Pamela Springsteen, sister of Bruce. By a strange quirk of fate, Springsteen was to release his two albums 'Lucky Town' and 'Human Touch' in America in the same week as Leppard released 'Adrenalize.'

Reviews had started to come in for the new album, and while gaining good reviews in Britain many American journals slated it, one going so far as to suggest that Leppard should quit immediately as they obviously have nothing left to offer. But, once again, the American public proved to be their saviours. 'Adrenalize' outsold Springsteen's two new releases and everything else. In America at least, it was acknowledged that that was who the band were up against. Whereas before they had been compared to Maiden or Whitesnake in terms of sales, now they were up against Whitney Houston and Janet Jackson. The one real rock band they were still compared to was Bon Jovi, who many feel snuck into the market place with Leppard soundalike songs while Leppard were away. Much of Bon Jovi's multi million selling album 'Slippery When Wet' owed plenty to Leppard, but rather than a rivalry Jon Bon Jovi and Joe were to become firm friends, although one bizarre incident when Bon Jovi played Dublin had Jon Bon Jovi looking at Joe "like a cat. I felt that I was being stalked by him." Jon later put this down to pre-concert nerves, but Joe was unsettled by it at the time It was probably partly due to Bon Jovi's success that Leppard were greeted more flatly when the album was released.

Apart from them there had been bands like Winger and Warrant who had taken elements of the Leppard sound without adding anything to it. Many people were beginning to get fed up with this slickness. Grunge had taken away all the glamour and posing from rock music, no bad thing, but Leppard were perceived as one of the standard bearers for this kind of band. Acts were dealing with this in different ways, the worst examples being those who put on a plaid shirt, grew a goatee and thought that no one would see through them, even though a year previously they had been swathed in spandex.

Leppard were suffering for the fact that their previous releases had broken new ground. Although 'Adrenalize' was not as strong as their previous two releases, it featured what were probably the best song titles they had ever come up with. 'Have You Ever Needed Someone So Bad' was marked out by several reviews in the non rock press as being a title that was wasted on 'this kind of rock music'. Just before they'd finished recording the album they had come up with the basics of a song called 'White Lightning' which was a memorial for Steve Clark and also one of the best songs they'd ever recorded. Joe was to say that the song was not so much a tribute as almost another form of catharsis. One of the main criticisms of the album was that it was too safe, whereas before they had always had a sense of adventure. Joe by now had mentioned several times that the band's songwriting yardstick were tracks such as; Queen's 'Bohemian Rhapsody' and The Beatles 'I Am The Walrus'.

to the idea that Mutt Lange had of listening to the classic rock songs of all time and trying to improve on them. Adult Orientated Radio was starting to be reviled in the States, and there were several swipes at the band because of their perceived love of this genre of music. One review summed up Leppard style of writing ballads as just a series of moody devises – serious guitar line, chorus harmony, and Joe's well meant but soul free vocals. Collen blamed all these criticisms on the rise of grunge. "A few years ago according to some papers we could do no wrong, now we sound out of date and old fashioned. We think that this is our best album so far, but we're at that stage in our career where people are just waiting to knock us. I've never felt like a dinosaur before." One interesting thing to note about the album was that in ultra conservative Korea the authorities banned the track 'Make Love Like A Man' on moral grounds, this meant that the album was released there consisting of only nine tracks. In South Africa the album's profits, like those of 'Hysteria' before it, were donated to South African charities.

BACK IN THE VILLAGE

W hile the rest of the world was worrying whether Leppard had stagnated, the band themselves were looking for a new guitarist. Collen had at one stage expressed a wish that they stay a single guitar band. He'd proved with the latest album that he didn't need another guitarist in the studio with him, and felt that with the new technology available he could do it all live too. He had also recently become the recipient of the ultimate accolade for guitarists, the Jackson guitar company producing a 'Jackson Phil Collen' guitar, and he was only the second person, after the late Randy Rhodes, to be given this accolade. Phil was instrumental in the making of this guitar, company boss Grover Jackson originally speaking to him when he went to Glenns Falls, New York where the band were rehearsing for the 'Hysteria' tour in 1987. Jackson remembered that the original drawing Phil had was of a guitar 'shaped like a lima bean.' The finished model has a radically arched body, giving it both distinctive sound and shape.

The rest of the band decided that they wanted to remain as a five piece, and Collen relented realising that he'd prefer the freedom of someone else to play off of, especially live. It was now that the rumour mill went into overdrive. One of the people mentioned was ex Iron Maiden guitarist Adrian Smith, who knew the band from their respective paths crossing throughout the years. Smith had all the criteria for Leppard, good vocals, good sense of humour, football player and above all, British. The band knew that they would be slated if they got an American guitarist in, in Britain at least where these kind of things are still seen as important, especially given the accusations that the band had to put up with about selling out to America a few years previously. He was offered the chance to audition, but decided against it. He'd left Maiden because he was sick of being away on tour so much, so what would be the point of joining a band like Leppard?

Another name mentioned was Collen's old guitar partner in Girl, Gerry Laffy.. Laffy says he was asked to learn some material and fly to Los Angeles to play with the band, but decided against it. "I wasn't the choice of everyone in the band, I think it was Phil egging everyone on that made them say they wanted me to fly over and play with them, plus I'd just finished work on a new album which I was really happy with ('Sublime To The Ridiculous, which featured Collen on a reworked version of the old Girl favourite 'Hollywood Tease') so when it came down to it I didn't bother getting on the plane!"

By far the strongest rumours concerned two people, John Sykes and Vivian Campbell. Sykes had been rumoured since Steve Clark was first having problems. He'd started his career in the Blackpool based band Streetfighter before joining the Tygers Of Pan Tang after turning up a week early for his audition and being sent home again. When he joined the Tygers Sykes was a massive rock fan, and once at the St Moritz club, after one of his first gigs with the Tygers Of Pan Tang, asked the then Michael Schenker Group singer Gary Bardens if he could have his t-shirt as a souvenir, which somewhat threw the singer who was later to wonder whether Sykes was joking. After the Tygers, Sykes had replaced Snowy White in Thin Lizzy, before being one of the many members of David Coverdale's hire 'em fire 'em vehicle Whitesnake, something he has in common with Campbell. Sykes was confirmed, in the press at least, as Leppard's new guitarist several times, but in the end all he contributed was some backing vocals to 'Adrenalize' along with Dave Steale from BB Steale. Sykes was also by now used to being a band leader with his own Blue Murder, whereas with Leppard he would have had to start as the new boy.

Campbell had no such leadership qualities, having been associated with bands with very strong personalities in David Coverdale and Ronnie James Dio. Originally from Ireland, he started with Sweet Savage, one of the bands that were swept along on the coat tails of the new wave of British heavy metal, a fairly unoriginal outfit but noted at the time for having a great guitarist; Campbell. Sweet Savage supported Thin Lizzy in Britain on the 'Renegade' tour, but apart from getting them known to a wider audience, it had no real effect on their stature. Campbell, who while on tour with Lizzy had been introduced to members of the press as 'a huge star of the future', already knew his ambitions lay beyond the band, and decided to take matters further when he read that Phil Collen was to leave Girl to join Def Leppard. Obtaining Phil Lewis's phone number wasn't difficult, as Lewis was an ambitious, and , contrary to his image, likeable person who would make his number fairly available to record industry people. Campbell brazenly offered his services to Lewis who informed him that Girl were not going to continue. Lewis said later that Girl were more of a close thing between him Collen and the Laffy brothers, Gerry and Simon, so once one of them went it was almost inevitable they would split. It was also obvious by this time that Girl wouldn't make it big, and something Lewis in particular was finding difficult to keep doing was to be the 'local hero' whose band could play the Marquee to a full audience of hangers on but were virtually fanless outside London.

Campbell was disappointed at the time, but realised that Girl were probably not the ideal band for him. He had also made his number freely available, and just under a month after his conversation with Lewis received a phone call from Jimmy Bain. Bain had played bass with Ritchie Blackmore's Rainbow and had formed a partnership with Brian Robertson in Wild Horses, a band which also featured Neil Carter who was to on to join UFO as a replacement for Paul Raymond. Wild Horses had supported Rush and Ted Nugent, but were not making any headway except, like Girl, among the hangers on and music industry liggers. Bain and Robertson's reputation as hard drinkers proceeded them, and Bain for one was sick of not being taken seriously as a musician any more. He'd received an offer to join up with Dio again, whom he had been with in Rainbow, and Dio was looking for a guitarist. Dio was adamant that he wanted someone new rather than an established player, and earlier that year Sweet Savage had supported Wild Horses, Bain not thinking much of the band but liking both Campbell's playing and ambition. "You could see he was in a different class" he says "and it was obvious someone was going to snap him up sooner or later, because I didn't think Sweet Savage were going to make it big and it was pretty obvious then that Vivian didn't either."

Campbell immediately upped to Los Angeles to join Dio, something which annoyed quite a few people back home in Ireland, though most people around the band knew that it was only a matter of time before he was off. Campbell confirmed his potential with Dio, and Ronnie felt slighted when he fairly quickly left to join Whitesnake. "I felt" he remembered later "as if I'd given him a big break but he didn't really repay me. Good luck to him, but I was left feeling let down.. It's OK now, but at the time I was felt slighted by him."

With Coverdale going through line up changes like there was no tomorrow, Campbell soon found himself out of the band, he went quickly from the short lived River Dogs to Shadow King with ex Foreigner frontman Lou Gramm. Shadow King were tipped as the next big thing for a while, but never seemed to make the good reviews turn into large crowds. Campbell, as one former colleague describes him, always had his eye on the main chance. "It was obvious as soon as Leppard got in contact he would go if he was given the opportunity" recalls one person who played with him "It seems like that's the way he's gone throughout his career, leaving as soon as something better comes along without any thought for those that get left behind." Unsurprisingly, this quote came from someone who was left behind.

Campbell was also working on a solo album for Epic records when Leppard got in contact, something he was asked to put aside when offered the position with Leppard. Of the guitarists that Leppard had asked over to rehearse with them, Campbell was the one that Collen felt most comfortable with. After such a close working relationship with Clark, this was very important. "Steve and I had different styles but really complimented each other, and when I started playing with Viv it felt natural, like it always had with Steve." The other important thing was the strength of Campbell's vocals. Clark had never sung live, partly due to a lack of confidence in his vocals, and Leppard had always multi tracked their vocals live, which they didn't like doing as this made the whole thing too sterile. They found that Campbell's voice blended in perfectly. It was some weeks after he'd joined that the official announcement was made, mainly due to the band wanting to be absolutely certain that he was right. "The social aspect was almost more important" said Elliot."We knew that we were going to be on tour for a long time and, to be honest, a few people could have fitted in musically. With Def Leppard you're very much a team player, so it's not like you were having to replace Eddie Van Halen or Ozzy Osbourne."

Oddly enough, at the same time Pete Willis re-emerged with a new outfit, Roadhouse. They signed to Vertigo, a subsidiary of the Phonogram label, and released an album and three singles including the well received 'Tower Of Love'. The songs were of undoubted quality, but they were to suffer by emerging just as the thrash and grunge movement was beginning to blur the lines of music, making it much harder for a band playing more 'conventional' rock music to gain an audience.

Leppard themselves decided to start touring immediately, once again using the 'in the round' stage. They decided on the name 'The Seven Day Weekend' tour. "We wanted something to reflect that we were a simple good time rock'n'roll band" says Elliot. "I sometimes feel that people are starting to look at us with a certain amount of sympathy, and that's the last thing we want. We want people to come along to our shows and forget the boring mundane things in their lives. It seems that so many bands are doom and gloom nowadays, but that's not us. I can't sing 'lets get rocked' one minute and 'let's not chop down the rainforests' the next. As worthy as that is, it's not Def Leppard and as soon as we started doing that people would see through us."

During this time, one of the band's heroes, Queen singer Freddie Mercury, died of AIDS and plans had been formulated for a tribute show/AIDS awareness day at Wembley Stadium. In a move that most bands wouldn't have

considered, Leppard chose this to be Campbell's debut with the band. The gig was to take place on Easter Monday 1992, and was shown live throughout the world on television with an estimated audience of nearly a billion people. The band were desperate to play it, even though with Campbell coming into the band, the timing couldn't have been worse. Collen thought it was important that they appeared. "It was to make people more aware, it wasn't a Def Leppard gig, but AIDS is something that loads of people are aware of but still (at the time of the gig) are convinced that it only happens to gays or needle users. We felt it was important for a conventional hard rock band like us to get involved."

Leppard's drum kit had been lost before they were due to go on stage, not normally a huge drawback but for Leppard this meant Ricks customised drums not being available. They were also unfortunate to go on after Metallica who had played a storming set. Leppard opened with 'Animal' and the sound was appalling. It was a band who hadn't played live before, and it showed. Afterwards they felt the gig did what it was supposed to do."It was the same when we did Donington in '86" recalled Joe. "Instead of coming back to a few gigs at two or three thousand seater venues we came back with a huge gig where we knew we would be judged. But we couldn't not get involved." For Joe, the highlight was singing backing vocals on a superb version of 'All The Young Dudes' with Ian Hunter and Mick Ronson, who by this time had been diagnosed as having cancer but was having something of a resurgence in popularity having been chosen to produce the album 'Your Arsenal' by ex Smiths singer and serious student of early seventies glam, Morrissey.

It was also at the Mercury tribute that Joe felt like grabbing Guns n' Roses bassist Steven Adler. He could see, as could millions of people on television, how completely out of it Adler was, and this coupled with his striking resemblance to Steve Clark made Joe want to slam him into the nearest wall. "I'm not some kind of father figure, but I could see so many similarities between the way he was behaving and the way Steve used to be. It was like watching it all happen again." Collen was later to remark that the Wembley appearance had been 'crap.' "If you wanted to present the band badly then that was the way to do it. It didn't matter, what mattered was the cause, but as a band it did us more harm than good."

Chapter Fifteen

'CAUSE THE BEST IS YET TO COME . . .

In the meantime, Q Prime management were busy setting up the 7 Day Weekend tour which would eventually last for fifteen months and take in 241 dates, 14 more than the Hysteria tour. The shows would once again take place in the round, but this time the band wanted to take the round stage to Britain, and in particular Earls Court in London. This had long been a wish of the band, especially Joe and Phil, due to the fact that this was where Led Zeppelin and Queen had played legendary concerts. The sheer weight of the staging had always meant that Leppard could not do this before, but now the staging was to be made of aluminium. After the disappointment of the Mercury tribute, there was talk that maybe Campbell wasn't the right man for Leppard, that maybe they were past their live performance best, that it was to much to expect them to reach the heights they had before.

Several articles following the Mercury tribute voiced the opinion that Leppard had become too much of an institution, that the exciting times were behind them. This did nothing to deter the ticket buying public. In Britain they played a Five venue tour, at the largest indoor arenas that Britain had to offer. Two nights at Earls Court, one of which took place on June 26th, the night of the final of the European Football Championships; a match that the band insisted was recorded for them so that they could watch it the minute they came off stage. Leppard were once again back to being a top class band.

The arrival of Campbell had hardly made any difference, even though he is a very different guitarist to Clark. In acknowledging Clark's death, Joe said they'd lost an old friend....and found a new one. Most nights of the tour Joe would blow a kiss to heaven in Steve's memory, but that was it. As Joe had said, no ceremony, no fanfare. Leppard also featured an acoustic interlude, with all but Allen sitting on stools playing guitars. On the American leg of the tour each member would improvise bits on his own, in a similar fashion to the way they had previously worked Creedence's 'Travellin' Band'. Some nights it would be Phil doing AC/DC's 'Back In Black', others Joe would play Nirvana's 'Smells Like Teen Spirit.' The mood on the tour was buoyant, especially as Leppard's pulling power in the States had remained fairly constant while others, including such big names as Kiss and Van Halen, had struggled badly. Joe was to remark more than once, that he felt Leppard were almost recession proof.

DEF LE

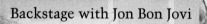
On stage with Brian May

Backstage with Jon Bon Jovi

DEF

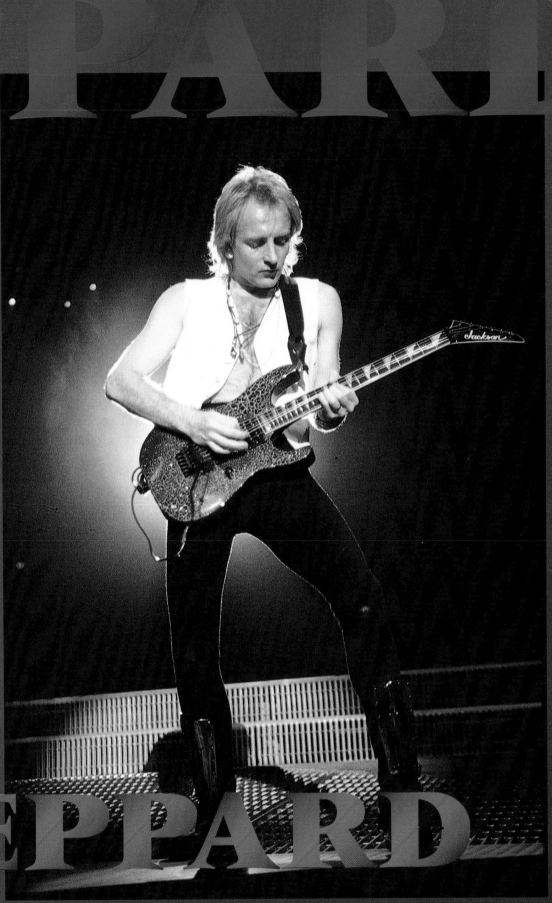

The date in Pittsburgh in November 1992 was almost cancelled when the band were informed that the staging, despite being lighter than it had been before, was too heavy to fly from the ceiling. Tony Diciocco from Q Prime management, like Mensch a smart, tough but polite operator (Mensch might have the reputation for being aggressive and shouting at people, but he could be unerringly helpful and extremely kind to those whom he felt were on his side) knew that Neil Diamond had played the same place just a few weeks previously and flown HIS equipment; Diciocco was informed that this was because he'd bought in his own support system, a contraption that looked like a giant upturned coffee table. The band decided that whatever it cost they'd hire the system from Diamond, a notorious showbiz scrooge. By the time they'd paid him, the profits from the show were to be fairly minimal, but at least they hadn't had to compromise. More seriously, later that same month, on a flight between gigs Joe thought he was having a heart attack, and a concerned crew radioed ahead and had him rushed to hospital as soon as the plane landed. Fortunately, his heart was fine but he had contracted pleurisy, the initial symptoms of which are similar to those of a cardiac arrest, and was told to rest for six weeks. This advice was ignored and Joe went on to play a gig that very evening with no ill effect, although he reported afterwards that he felt a little more tired than usual.

During the tour the Mayor of Fargo, who's daughter was a big Def Leppard fan, declared 1st September 'Def Leppard Day', and the band had their hand prints (except in Allen's case, who provided a boot print) immortalised on the Fargo Walk Of Fame. The band had also had in mind plans for a big outdoor show in their hometown of Sheffield. They'd played Sheffield Arena on the British Leg of their tour, but wanted to do a proper, big home gig. "It's always been our ambition to play a show in Britain like we do in the States" declared Joe at the time. "Even in Germany on the this (the 7 Day Weekend) tour we've headlined a show to over fifty five thousand people. It has to be in Sheffield, and I wanted to play it at Bramall Lane." This being the home of Sheffield United, Sav would not play there. Joe wouldn't play at Sheffield Wednesday's Hillsborough ground. Finally a compromise was reached and the band settled on the Don Valley Stadium.

On the 6th June 1993 they, along with support from British rock band Thunder, played what Joe was to describe as one of the finest gigs they'd ever done. "It was, in the strangest way, like we'd finally made it. A big home gig in front of a big crowd, the kind of thing I used to dream of along with scoring the winning goal in the F.A. Cup Final. " The tour finally ended in Mexico, where Joe had caused so much offence ten years previously, with the band playing to over 20,000 people. They were to remember this gig with enthusiasm, as the Mexican crowd were completely wild. "It felt" said Collen "like they'd never seen a rock band before. The vibe was so strong. It's almost as if they're not tainted by fashion that they like what they like rather than what they think is in at the time. It was definitely a great place to finish."

The band had also finally got around to releasing the much talked about collection of rarities, demos and outtakes, an idea that had been kicking around since 1987 when Mutt Lange remarked that 'Ring Of Fire' the b-side of "Armageddon It' was too good to languish there and should be released on the next album. Originally intended more as a souvenir for fans, Leppard released 'Two Steps Behind' a song that had originally appeared in acoustic form on the 12" version of 'Make Love Like A Man'. This time an electric version was released, and much to everyone's surprise it became the bands biggest selling single ever. This set the tone for the album, to be called 'Retro Active, the cover of which at first looked like a skull but is in fact a woman sitting at a dressing table, her head reflected back to form the right eye socket of the skull. It garnered excellent reviews, and rather than the souvenir it was intended to be, it became a bone fide album. Joe said part of the reason for releasing it was something he called the 'Status Quo factor'. "Everyone reckoned they knew what we would be releasing next, how it would sound. We've always thought our stuff was consistent, and this isn't the case with 'Retro active. It's definitely our most varied album." From the ultra heavy 'Desert Song' to Joe playing piano on 'Miss You In A Heartbeat' he was proved right. It was also an interesting contrast to have 'Ride Into The Sun' on the album, and many viewed it as a closing of a huge chapter of the bands career. The band also included 'I Wanna Be Your Hero', which was on the soundtrack for the Arnold Schwatzeneger film 'The Last Action Hero'; and a version of a song that Joe had long felt to be a neglected classic, the Sweet song 'Action'. This song once again took them into the British singles charts and gave them another appearance on Top Of The Pops'.

After the tour Sav got married in Dublin, while Joe went to New York to record his part on a tribute album to Mick Ronson. He also organised a benefit concert at the Hammersmith Apollo, formerly the Odeon, for the anniversary of Ronson's death, featuring ex members of David Bowie's backing band The Spiders From Mars and Ian Hunter. It felt strange to him that now HE was the main person behind this, the one who could get all his former heroes mobilised in this way.

They also started writing material with Campbell for the first time, Joe declaring it to be brilliant. "Just having another dimension to the writing, someone else's input for the first time for over ten years is making it fresher. When we wrote 'Hysteria' we wanted it to sound like 1997, with 'Adrenanlize' we were going for the year 2000. For the first time we consciously want it to sound current." The suicide of Nirvana's Kurt Cobain in April of 1994 also, in an oblique way, referred to the band. The final line of his suicide note was the line the band had borrowed from Neil Young's 'Hey, Hey My, My', in 'Rock Of Ages', "It's better to burn out than fade away."

After all that's happened to them, Leppard remain an inventive and creative rock force. One with a more interesting history than most, but one with a sense of togetherness and purpose that has seen them through. The future, once again, looks bright, but as they themselves say on the 'Adrenalize' album cover . . .

"Only one thing is certain . . . . . . Nothing."

DISCOGRAPHY

JANUARY 1979 SRTS/78/CUS/232 BLUDGEON RIFFOLA

RIDE INTO THE SUN

GETCHA ROCKS OFF

OVERTURE

Def Leppard's first ever vinyl release. 1000 copies only released.
Only 150 originally issued with cover and signed lyric sheet.

MAY 1979 MSB001 BLUDGEON RIFFOLA

RIDE INTO THE SUN

GETCHA ROCKS OFF

OVERTURE

15,000 copies only issued.

DISCOGRAPHY

UK SINGLES

CAT. No.	FORMAT	TITLE	RELEASED
6059 240	7"	**GETCHA ROCKS OFF** / Ride Into The Sun / The Overture	Sept '79
6059 247	7"	**WASTED** / Hello America	17 Nov '79
LEPP 1	7"	**HELLO AMERICA** / Good Morning Freedom	21 Feb '80
LEPP 2	7"	**LET IT GO** / Switch 625 *(free patch included with first 10,000)*	Aug '81
LEPP 3	7"	**BRINGIN' ON THE HEARTBREAK** / Me And My Wine	
LEPP 312	12"	Bringin' On The Heartbreak	
		Me And My Wine / You Got Me Runnin'	13 Nov '81
VER 5	7"	**PHOTOGRAPH** / Bringin' On The Heartbreak	
VERP 5	7"	Photograph / Bringin' On The Heartbreak *("pop up" sleeve)*	
VERX 5	12"	Photograph / Bringin' On The Heartbreak	
		Mirror Mirror (Look Into My Eyes)	3 Feb '83
VER 6	7"	**ROCK OF AGES** / Action! Not Words	
VERP 6	7"	Rock Of Ages / Action! Not Words *(shaped picture disc)*	
VERQ 6	7"	Rock Of Ages / Action! Not Words *("fold out" pack)*	
VERX 6	12"	Rock Of Ages / Action! Not Words	20 May '83
VER 8	7"	**TOO LATE FOR LOVE** / Foolin'	
VERX 8	12"	Too Late For Love / Foolin' / High 'n' Dry (Saturday Night)	25 Nov '83
VER 9	7"	**PHOTOGRAPH** (re-release) / Bringin' On The Heartbreak	
VERG 9	7"	Photograph / Bringin' On The Heartbreak *(gatefold sleeve)*	
VERX 9	12"	Photograph / Bringin' On The Heartbreak	
		Mirror Mirror (Look Into My Eyes)	17 Feb '84
LEP 1	7"	**ANIMAL** / Tear It Down	
LEPXM 1	MCSP	Animal (Extended Version) / Animal / Tear It Down	
LEPX 1	12"	Animal (Extended Version) / Animal / Tear It Down	20 July '87
LEP 2	7"	**POUR SOME SUGAR ON ME** / I Wanna Be Your Hero	
LEPS 2	7"	Pour Some Sugar On Me / I Wanna Be Your Hero *(shaped picture disc)*	
LEPMC 2	MCSP	Pour Some Sugar On Me (Extended Version) / Pour Some Sugar On Me	
		I Wanna Be Your Hero	
LEPX 2	12"	Pour Some Sugar On Me (Extended Version)	
		Pour Some Sugar On Me / I Wanna Be Your Hero	14 Sept '87

DISCOGRAPHY

UK SINGLES

CAT. No.	FORMAT	TITLE	RELEASED
LRP 3	7"	**HYSTERIA** / Ride Into The Sun	
LEPS 3	7"	Hysteria / Ride Into The Sun *(with free patch)*	
LEP 333	MCSP	Hysteria / Ride Into The Sun / Love And Affection (live)	
LEPX 3	12"	Hysteria / Ride Into The Sun / Love And Affection (live)	
LEPCD 3	CDSP	Hysteria / Ride Into The Sun / Love And Affection (live)	
		I Wanna Be Your Hero	23 Nov '87
LEP 4	7"	**ARMAGEDDON IT** / Ring Of Fire	
LEPP 4	7"	Armageddon It / Ring Of Fire *(poster bag)*	
LEPX 4	12"	Armageddon It ('88 Ext. Mix) / Ring Of Fire / Armageddon It	
LEPXB 4	12"	Armageddon It ('88 Ext. Mix) / Ring Of Fire	
		Armageddon It (Album Version) *(boxed single with poster & cards)*	
LEPCD 4	CDSP	Armageddon It (Album Version) / Ring Of Fire / Animal	
		Pour Some Sugar On Me	March '88
LEP 5	7"	**LOVE BITES** / Billy's Got A Gun (live)	
LEPG 5	7"	Love Bites / Billy's Got A Gun (live) *(gatefold sleeve with booklet)*	
LEPX 5	12"	Love Bites / Billy's Got A Gun (live) / Excitable (The Orgasmic Mix)	
LEPXB 5	12"	Love Bites / Billy's Got A Gun (live) / Excitable (The Orgasmic Mix)	
		(boxed single with cards)	
LEPCD 5	CDSP	Love Bites / Rocket (The Lunar Mix) / Billy's Got A Gun (live)	May '88
LEP 6	7"	**ROCKET** / Release Me	
LEPC 6	7"	Rocket / Release Me *(calendar pack)*	
LEPX 6	12"	Rocket (The Lunar Mix) / Release Me / Rock Of Ages (live)	
LEPXP 6	12"	Rocket (The Lunar Mix) / Rocket (Radio Edit)	
		Release Me *(picture disc)*	
LEPXC 6	12"	Rocket (The Lunar Mix) / Release Me	
		Rock Of Ages (live) *(calendar pack)*	
LEPCD 6	CDSP	Rocket (The Lunar Mix) / Rock Of Ages (live) / Release Me	Jan '89
DEF 7	7"	**LET'S GET ROCKED** / Only After Dark	
DEFMC 7	MCSP	Let's Get Rocked / Only After Dark	
DEFXP 7	12"	Let's Get Rocked / Only After Dark	
		Too Late For Love (live) *(picture disc)*	
DEFCD 7	CDSP	Let's Get Rocked / Only After Dark	
		Woman (live) *(boxed CD)*	23 March '92

DISCOGRAPHY

UK SINGLES

CAT. No.	FORMAT	TITLE	RELEASED
LEP 7	7"	**MAKE LOVE LIKE A MAN** / Miss You In A Heartbeat	
LEPMC 7	MCSP	Make Love Like A Man / Miss You In A Heartbeat	
LEPXP 7	12"	Make Love Like A Man / Miss You In A Heartbeat / Two Steps Behind (Acoustic Version) *(picture disc)*	
LEPCB 7	CDSP	Make Love Like A Man / Miss You In A Heartbeat / Action Two Steps Behind (Acoustic Version) *(picture CD)*	June '92
LEP 8	7"	**HAVE YOU EVER NEEDED SOMEONE SO BAD** / From The Inside	
LEPMC 8	MCSP	Have You Ever Needed Someone So Bad / From The Inside	
LEPXP 8	12"	Have You Ever Needed Someone So Bad / From The Inside / You Can't Always Get What You Want *(picture disc)*	
LEPCB 8	CDSP	Have You Ever Needed Someone So Bad / From The Inside / You Can't Always Get What You Want / Little Wing	Sept '92
LEP 9	7"	**HEAVEN IS** / She's Too Tough *(autographed etched disc)*	
LEPMC 9	MCSP	Heaven Is / She's Too Tough	
LEPX 9	12"	Heaven Is / She's Too Tough / Let's Get Rocked (live)	
LEPCD 9	CDSP	Heaven Is / She's Too Tough / Elected (live) Let's Get Rocked (live)	Jan '93
LEP 10	7"	**TONIGHT** / Now I'm Here (live)	
LEPMC 10	MCSP	Tonight / Now I'm Here (live)	
LEPPCD 10	CDSP	Tonight / Now I'm Here (live) / Photograph (live)	
LEPCB 10	CDSP	Tonight / Pour Some Sugar On Me (live) Tonight (demo) *(CD "Z" pack)*	
LEPXP 11	12"	Tonight / Now I'm Here (live) / Hysteria (live) *(picture disc)*	April '93
LEPMC 12	MCSP	**TWO STEPS BEHIND** / Tonight	
LEPCD 12	CDSP	Two Steps Behind / Tonight / SMC	
LEPTN 12	CDSP	Two Steps Behind / Tonight / SMC *(CD in embossed metal tin)*	Sept '93
LEP 13	7"	**ACTION** / Miss You In A Heartbeat (Phil's Demo)	
LEPMC 13	MCSP	Action / Miss You In A Heartbeat (Phil's Demo)	
LEPCD 13	CDSP	Action / She's Too Tough (Joe's Demo) Miss You In A Heartbeat (Phil's Demo)	
LEPCX 13	CDSP	Action / Two Steps Behind (Joe's Demo) / Love Bites (live from Don Valley Stadium, Sheffield) *(digipack with discography)*	Jan '94

DISCOGRAPHY

ALBUMS

CAT. No.	LABEL	RELEASE DATE	TITLE
6360180	Vertigo	March 1980	**ON THROUGH THE NIGHT**
6359045	Vertigo	July 1981	**HIGH 'N' DRY**
VERS2 (6359119)	Vertigo	February 1983	**PYROMANIA**
HYSLP1 (830 675-1)	Bludgeon Riffola Phonogram	August 1987	**HYSTERIA**
HYSLPD 1	Bludgeon Riffola Phonogram	December 1987	**HYSTERIA** *Special "Picture Disc" version of album*
510 978-1	Bludgeon Riffola Phonogram	March 1992	**ADRENALIZE**
514 256-1	Bludgeon Riffola Phonogram	December 1992	**ADRENALIZE** *Special "Picture Disc" version of album* includes bonus tracks "She's Too Tough" & "Miss You In A Heartbeat"
518 215-1	Bludgeon Riffola Phonogram	October 1993	**RETROACTIVE**